Walking Through Clear Water
in a Pool Painted Black

Walking Through Clear Water
in a Pool Painted Black

COOKIE MUELLER

SEMIOTEKT(E) NATIVE AGENTS SERIES

Special thanks to Kim Spurlock and Scott Covert

Copyright © 1990 Semiotext(e)
Semiotext(e)
PO Box 629
South Pasadena, CA 91031

Printed in the United States of America

We gratefully acknowledge
financial assistance in the
publication of this book from the
New York State Council on the Arts.

ISBN 978-0-936756-61-5
10 9 8 7 6

CONTENTS

Two People — Baltimore — 1964

I had two lovers and I wasn't ashamed. The first was Jack. He was seventeen and I was fifteen. The skin of his face was so taut over protruding bones that I feared for his head, the same sympathetic fear one has for the safety of an egg.

He wore his black hair all greased up with pieces spiralling down into his languid eyes. Jack owned only black clothes, and he wore his cigarettes in the rolled up sleeves of his black tee-shirts, showing off his solid pecks which were big for a skinny person.

Once I visited him in the hospital; he had infectious hepatitis and sclerosis of the liver, resulting from his four year bout with alcoholism.

He didn't look too good in there, all yellow in a murky blue private room.

His visitors had to wear hospital gowns and surgical gloves, also masks over their nose and mouths which really frustrated him because everyone looked so morose, and sinister without smiles.

My nose and lips were the first nose and lips he had seen in two weeks… after his mother left I whipped off not only my mask and gown, but my pants, and hopped into the hospital bed with him. I wasn't afraid. I'd been as intimate as I could be right up until the time he got sick, but I kept my rubber gloves on anyway.

He was very sick, quite contagious, and looked ill, but sexy, like pictures of Proust on his deathbed. I was in love, and we were teenagers going steady.

He had been expelled from high school for bringing in real moonshine, corn liquor, from his uncle's still in West Virginia, and he'd gotten all his best friends drunk on the lunch break and tried to beat up on his American history teacher when the man had dumped out Jack's liquor.

Jack had a black Impala convertible with red rolled and pleated bucket seats, racing cams, dual exhausts, tire slicks, a roll bar, Laker pipes, big foam dice hanging from the rear view mirror, and four on the floor, of course.

He drank Sloe Gin, or Laird's Apple Jack, or sometimes Thunderbird when he couldn't find anything else. He ate bennies (Benzedrine) like little candies. He called them cross-roads because of the X on them.

This other lover of mine was Gloria. She sat three rows in front of me in Algebra class. I watched her hair-dos from the back. Everyday they were different: Beehives, Barrelcurls, Air-Lifts, Pixies, flips, French Twists, Bubbles, Doublebubbles.

The things I liked best were the way her scalp shone through all the teasing as if her head was a mango and the spit curls pasted down beside her ears with clear finger nail polish. She also had bitten-to-the-quick fingernails. I even liked the warts and nicotine stains on her index and second fingers. On her, all this was heaven.

I began spending Saturday nights with Gloria when Jack had bloody cut eyes from fights. When he went in the hospital, I stayed with her the whole weekend. I slept in her single bed at her pre-fab parent's house and first she used to feel me up. She kept telling me, "Just pretend I'm Jack. Just pretend I'm Jack."

In the beginning the cajoling was necessary, but in the weeks that followed I didn't have to pretend she was Jack anymore.

Jack and Gloria liked each other and no one ever suspected anything about Gloria and myself. For appearances, we were best girlfriends, both of us with our combustible hairdos, sprayed with lacquer and teased high as possible. We wore the tightest black skirts… so tight that they hobbled us… black stockings, white blouses with ruffles at the neck and cuffs, pointy bras underneath and five inch spike heels. With these shoes, and the hair, we were the tallest people in the school. Lesser women than we would have become acrophobic. We made people dizzy when they saw us.

We clicked down the high school hallways in our spikes, these shoes I had to keep in my school locker to change into when I got there in the mornings... my mother made me wear flats to school.

When Jack was in the hospital, we picked up guys together, smoked a lot of cigarettes, sniffed glue, and drank codeine terpenhydrate cough syrup for the buzz.

I stopped seeing Jack and took his initial ring off when he went to jail for a B and E (breaking and entering) charge. I stopped seeing Gloria when she got pregnant and decided to marry Ed, her long time boyfriend, who she kept telling me she didn't love nearly as much as she loved me.

Years later, I found out that Jack, who was always pretty literate, was on methadrine writing a novel, never able to drink again because of his liver.

As for Gloria... that girl... born of a light bulb it seemed, had died when she had gotten silicone injections for her little tits. It had spread all over her body making tiny lumps arise on every inch of her skin, until finally it entered her pulmonary arteries and the aorta and she died of a silicone heart.

Haight Ashbury — San Francisco — 1967

An earthquake rolled me off the mattress onto the floor. It woke me along with the rest of San Francisco. It was nothing too unusual considering the San Andreas fault; there were a lot of houses all over the city that were crooked from past tremors. This one was 5.6 on the Richter scale at 10 a.m., an uncivilized hour.

It was too early to get up, but I decided I couldn't sleep any longer in the same bed with this person who I liked just fine yesterday when we liberated two T-bone steaks from the Safeway supermarket which we cooked and ate, much to the disgust of the vegetarians I lived with. After the steaks we drank a gallon of cheap Napa Sonoma red wine and took some LSD... Owsley Purple Barrels. But now he was sweating too much in bed, staining the one sheet I owned with all that wasted power from his pores. It meant he couldn't hold his liquor or his drugs, which irritated me so much I had to escape.

I went to the bathroom quietly so I wouldn't wake the eleven people I lived with. My roommates were spread out among five bedrooms. five, if you consider the glassed in porch off the kitchen that overlooked the dismal cement courtyard. We shared this courtyard with another building where Janis Joplin from Big Brother And The Holding Company lived. On some mornings I could see her rattling her pots and pans in her kitchen. Sometimes we'd talk across the concrete abyss like housewives.

I put on my eye makeup. It was a throwback to the time when I plastered the makeup on thick and teased my hair. No one else wore eye makeup in the Haight... an occasional Dayglow flower or a third eye on the forehead perhaps, but definitely no eye makeup. Then I went out on Haight Street looking for something new.

The first thing I saw was a school bus painted black with the words HOLYWOOD PRODUCTIONS (one L was missing in Hollywood) scrawled in gold by what must have been a retarded person. A tall hambone was sitting on the bus stairs. I asked him for a cigarette, just to strike up a conversation. I was curious.

"No cigarettes," he said, "but why don't you come in and smoke a joint with us?"

I followed him in and sat down among paisley throw pillows, bare mattresses and hanging sand candles. The interior was painted sky blue with splashes of red. five or six girls were lounging inside. They looked my age, but seemed younger. Maybe it was their dull eyes, maybe it was their girlie prattle, but they seemed like boring people, dressed like hippies. They were like ducks quacking over corn. I immediately felt superior. There was something missing here, faulty brain synapses, low wattage cerebral electrodes, maybe.

After we all smoked the joint and talked a little, one of the girls asked, "Would you like to join us? We're travelling up and down the coast in this bus." Everyone thought it was a good idea if I joined them. I thought it was rather sudden; I met them three minutes ago, but these people were weaned into peace and free love straight from their parent's Wonderbread and Cheese Doodles, so they were disgustingly enthusiastic.

I tried to picture myself travelling "up and down" the coast with them but my blood turned cold.

"I don't think so," said I. "I have a flat here with eleven other people so I'm sort of set up, you know? What's the situation on this bus? I mean, how many of you are there?"

"There's eight right now. Six girls and two guys. You should really wait for Charlie to come back from the store before you decide. He's really far out and spiritual. He's in there buying oranges for us." She pointed to a fruit store.

I waited around for a little while, but then decided to leave, so I thanked them for the joint and left looking for a diversion from this bunch. It wasn't until years later while reading *The Family* that I remembered that bus. It was described in the book exactly as I remembered it. Those girls were Squeaky Fromme, Susan Atkins, Mary Brunner... I just missed meeting Charlie Manson by five minutes.

Next on the street I noticed a gathering of women. I thought this was a little odd since this was long before the days when women felt it their duty to exclude men from their conversations. As I got closer, I realized the blond in the center of the group was extolling the virtues of Jimi Hendrix, after having fucked him the night before. I walked on by. It seemed silly. I'd fucked him the night before she had.

I moved on to Golden Gate Park. As usual, the sky over Hippie Hill was dark with frisbees, kites and seagulls. Hundreds of hippie's dogs were barking and walking on people laying on the grass. The air was thick with the smell of marijuana, patchouli oil, jasmine incense and Eucalyptus trees. Black guys were playing congos and flutes; white guys were playing harmonicas and guitars. It was as crowded as Coney Island on the Fourth of July. Hippie Hill was like this every day of the week.

I ran into some friends and sat around drinking wine. Noonish, I stopped back at 1826 Page Street, my home. An LSD capping party was in progress. It was the sort of party that only happened where an acid dealer lived.

The object of the party was to put LSD powder into gelatin capsules, but since the LSD assimilated through the skin, everyone got pretty high. The party went on in shifts. When someone got too high to continue, another person would take their place. So when Kirk, one of my roommates, dropped out, I took his place in front of a large mound of white powder. After filling about 300 capsules, I felt that familiar surge of LSD. Soon I didn't care about capping LSD anymore, and besides my fingers weren't doing my bidding. Someone took my place and I went back out on the street.

I walked down Page Street, which runs parallel to Haight. The sidewalk was now lined with hippies and dealers trying to sell anything you might want to get high.

I was high enough, and Haight Street was too crowded for me. So I went back to Page Street and walked to the Catholic church where I could be alone. It was empty except for an old lady in a pew who didn't notice me. It was near Easter, so the alter was dressed in purple and gold. It was peaceful.

Since I wasn't raised Catholic, the confessional booths had always fascinated me. I looked into them. There were booths on both sides of the priest's box, but the priest's box looked the best. It had a velvet armchair and gold and purple raiments hung over the backrest. The booth was bathed in blue light. On LSD it looked so comforting… a great spot to sit for awhile, so holy. I went in and closed the door. I was tripping my brains out so even if I had been a Catholic I wouldn't have thought this was a weird thing to do at the time.

A minute later the door opened. I thought at first it must be the priest, but no, it was some jerk. Maybe it was the janitor or someone like that, there to tell me to leave, but no, he fell to his knees in the cramped space. His glasses fogged up. He began sweating.

"Let me eat you," he whispered. "Please let me eat you."

Woah, was this guy a pervert! This was disgusting. Who could think about sex on LSD in a confessional booth? I was feeling like a flaccid fungus, totally unsexy.

Where had this guy materialized from? He wasn't in the church when I came in.

I said something like, "No, my son, but you're forgiven. Go now in peace." I made the sign of the cross. But he didn't leave. He got physical, but I climbed over him and bolted out the door, past the pews and back into the eye-damaging sunlight of the street.

A flatbed truck came lumbering toward me, carrying amplifiers, guitars, drums, a group of hippies and THE GRATEFUL DEAD. They stopped, extended a hand and pulled me onboard. We were on our way to San Quentin to give a free concert for the prisoners. Not much happened out there, but the music was good and the prisoners liked it.

By the time I reached home, everybody was snorting heroin to come down from the acid capping party. I helped myself to some and laid down for a bit.

A friend named Patrick, who I hadn't seen in awhile stopped by. He woke me and talked me into visiting his new guru, Anton LaVey, America's foremost demonologist and devil worshipper of the moment. It sounded interesting, so I went. First we stopped at Patrick's sister's house to borrow her car. She was having what appeared to be a sit-down dinner for a bunch of American Indians. What it turned out to be wasn't a dinner at all, but an authentic peyote ceremony. Her husband, a full-blooded Sioux, was munching on some peyote buttons. They all were. They offered us some; we ate them; they were nauseating. The Indians reminded us that we had to return the next day to drink each other's urine so we could get high all over again. It was part of the three-day ceremony.

"Oh, I'll be back," I lied. Are they joking? Drink the piss of those fat wrinkled Indians? Anyway what were they doing have a peyote ceremony sitting around on plastic chairs, in a pre-fab apartment, wearing polyester flowered shirts under fluorescent lights? Weren't they supposed to be out on the plains, under the stars wearing buffalo pelts? Their ancestors were probably rolling over in their sacred burial grounds.

When we got to LaVey's formidable Victorian house, which was painted black, all of it, down to the drainpipes and the ornate woodwork, Patrick asked me to sit in the livingroom and wait for him to return.

The livingroom looked like a film set for Poe's story *The Fall of the House of Usher.* LaVey entered wearing velvet robes. He seemed surprisingly cordial and human. He brought some sort of liquid for me to drink. Patrick returned carrying a bag. LaVey nodded to Patrick and left.

"We're going to have some fun now, Cookie," he said. "We're going to Mount Tamalpais to evoke one of Beelzebub's footmen. Whataya say?"

"Fine with me. Let's go." I was pretty sure LaVey was a fraud supported by naive fools like Patrick... although... at the same time I couldn't dismiss the creepy feeling I got inside the house.

As we crossed the Golden Gate Bridge, Patrick told me he had personally performed a black ceremony that resulted in the *San Francisco Chronicle* newspaper strike. I decided Patrick was nuts.

The summit of Mount Tamalpais was entirely too dark. There was hardly a moon that night and the trees, rocks, even my own feet beneath me were looking distorted. It seemed like spirits had invaded, making everything undulate and change shape. Maybe the knowledge this spot had been a sacred burial ground had to do with those sensations.

Patrick opened his bag and produced a bloodstone talisman, a jar of blood, a black-handled knife, a bag of herbs, the hooves of a goat and a black book. He scratched a nine foot circle and a pair of pentacles in the dirt. After seeing all this, I began suspecting Patrick might be dangerous. I knew enough from books about the black arts to realize when someone was taking themself too seriously.

When clouds began moving across the crescent moon it got so dark that the edge of the mountain disappeared and the earth beneath my feet was no longer visible. Patrick told me to stand in the middle of the circle. He said I would be okay since this was the protected spot. I thought, if this was the protected spot, why wasn't Patrick standing there with me? But I stepped inside the circle anyway and Patrick began reading from his black book. Just as I was beginning to relax, sure this was all ridiculous, I heard something in the distance running towards us. I heard footsteps and a screeching voice, half-human, half-animal. I was not imagining. Maybe it was a big wounded flightless bird? What else had only two feet in the animal kingdom? This thing certainly sounded like it was on two feet, not four.

I tried to categorize the sound... but fear overtook reason. I felt my body cold. My stomach sank. I felt like I must be going ashen. The little hairs on my body rose and waved like wheat in the wind. For the first time I knew the feeling of one's hair standing on end. I looked at Patrick, who was obviously not in command of the situation. He looked like someone being disemboweled. I guess he hadn't expected such dramatic results either.

If this was a test of courage, I lost. If this was a ritual for human sacrifice with me as the victim, I won, because I didn't wait around to find out. I couldn't stand it. No one with a shred of sanity would have been able to stand there.

So I ran, I left Patrick in the dust like the roadrunner in cartoons. I ran faster than I ever had in my life, probably crossed paths with the footman himself, jumped into the car, took the keys from under the floor mat and tore down the side of the mountain, tires squealing around the narrow precarious curves, gunning it full blast to the Golden Gate Bridge. When I finally saw the bridge lights (fear had altered my vision I think), the superstructure was melting and the houses on the other side were disintegrating. The road rose and fell like storm swells on the sea. I wanted to scream to the passersby but they looked shockingly inhuman. I kept feeling like there was someone or something in the back seat with me.

When I got home, I leapt out of the car and ran inside so scared that everyone was horrified (most of them were on THC and STP). They calmed down, and I calmed down. I took a hot bath and relaxed.

A little later we all decided to use Patrick's car and go out to Berkeley to see Jim Morrison play at some ballroom there. We wanted to distribute the Blue Cheer LSD that had gone through the laundry by accident. Susan had stashed it in the dirty laundry the day before. Mark hadn't known and washed the whole load (about $400 worth of the stuff) with the detergent Cheer. Now the whole batch of LSD was Blue Cheer and Cheer combined. We planned to give it away free, providing of course people didn't mind the accompanying side effects of the detergent.

Jim Morrison was good, as usual, and so was the LSD, despite the slight stomach cramps. We even handed a lump of the goo to him onstage and he happily ate it. After the concert, we left to smoke opium at home, leaving Kathy and Eve to go backstage to try and fuck Morrison. While smoking opium and listening to KMPX (the best radio station at the time), we heard an unfamiliar song. It was great, unlike anything else we'd ever heard. I offered, since we didn't have a phone, to go out into the three a.m. morning and call KMPX and get the title and the name of the musician.

While I was in the phone booth, after I talked to the KMPX D.J. and found out it was a cut from a new album, *Doctor John the Night Tripper,* a black man with short hair walked up and stood next to the booth. I thought he was waiting to use the phone, but no, it was me he was waiting for.

"How do you like Stokely Carmichael?" he asked.

"He's okay. I don't really care one way or the other about him, to tell you the truth," I said, unsure of the relevance of the question.

"Would you like to meet him?"

"Not right now. It's a little late, don't you think? He's probably asleep," I answered.

But he drew a gun from inside an Iceberg Slim book. I looked around feebly for help. There was none.

"Come with me and we'll meet him," he said. He took me to his Lincoln and we got in.

We never met Stokely Carmichael.

Actually it would have been nicer to meet him because this turned out to be rape. It wasn't even done well and he was stupid besides, just like the young girls on the Manson bus. But he did give me a gift from his large glove compartment... a musical jewelry box, the kind that has the ballerina in the pink tutu.

I ingeniously cajoled him to drive me back into my neighborhood by asking him to come home with me. I knew there'd be people walking around on the streets in the Haight, so I could just jump out of the car when he stopped at a red light or something. I told him I had wall-to-wall carpeting, air conditioning, a huge color TV set and heroin waiting for him. When we got to the Haight, I saw a few hippies walking by, so I flung the door open, and clutching the music box, threw myself out of the moving car.

"That man just raped me," I screamed to them. They pounced on the car and pulled the guy out. There was a resident's hippie vigilante group forming in the Haight at the time, and these were some of them. They were taking the law into their own hands, to protect "their womenfolk" from things just like this. They didn't beat the guy up. Hippies didn't do that kind of thing. They gave him a big dose of LSD instead and took his gun away from him.

When I got home, a bit shaken once again, everyone was doing cocaine mixed with crystal methadrine. They got upset for a minute when I told them the rape story. Kirk asked me why I was always the one to have all the fun.

They offered me some cocaine and methadrine and we ushered in the dawn talking about aesthetics, Eastern philosophy, Mu, Atlantis, and the coming apocalypse. We recorded the conversation, not realizing we were all making the same points five or six times. It would sound foolishly cyclical the next day.

But it was already the next day... time for me to go back out on Haight Street and have some more fun.

The Pig Farm — Baltimore & York, PA — 1969

I was shopping for knockwurst, but it was the end of the day for the butchers at the A&P, and they were breaking down the meat section, so I settled for a package of frozen breakfast links. This was when I first saw Herb Eickerman watching me from the produce section, apathetically fingering the potatoes. He looked like a young blond Robert Mitchum, the hooded eyes, the unforgiving jaw, well worn Levis, muscles.

His expression changed the minute he saw me go for the frozen links. He approached me and put his hand on my package.

"Them sausages ain't no good," he said with a voice like Johnny Cash.

"Oh yeah?" I said, irritated. Who was this guy? "Are you an Oscar Myer wiener salesman or something?"

"Those thangs are frozen even," he tried to pull the links from my hand, "I know pigs and these ain't from good pigs."

"One person's opinion," I said callously, thinking that this was a low display of meat sabotage. At this, the links slipped from his grip; his determination fizzled. I tossed my frozen links into my cart and wheeled away thinking about this man, this pork devotee. Maybe he was just one of those familiar cruisers, the grocery singles types, picking up girls in the meat section.

A moment later I ran into Bob, a friend known as the Psychedelic Pig because he was fat, he sold LSD and had a huge collection of ceramic pigs: stuffed pigs, wooden pigs, pig clocks, pig lamps. His whole house was a porker menagerie.

He was there at the A&P with a cart full of Pepsi, club soda, beer, potato chips, dips, cakes, pies, donuts. It looked like he was having a party. He was, he told me.

"The main course is a roast suckling piglet," he laughed. "A friend of mine who owns a pig farm gave me the pig for the dinner. Isn't that perfect?"

"A pig farm?" I asked.

"He's around here somewhere helping me shop," he glanced around. "You're coming to my party, right? I thought you knew. It's my birthday."

When I got to the party, I found, as I had suspected, the blond Robert Mitchum was the pig farmer in question.

So... he actually did know something about pigs. This gave him credibility. He got more handsome at the party.

We talked. He was shy.

He told me that near York, Pennsylvania he had a 9,000 acre farm… land that had been in his family for generations, when his great great grandfather had left Austria with his famous opera star wife, a balding coloratura soprano who kept lots of wigs and pearls. This was Herb's great great grandmother. He was very proud of his mother's side.

We left the party together to sit on the edge of the Baltimore Harbor, and watch the sun sink on the Domino Sugar Refinery and the harbor's greasy water. With the sun bouncing red on the waves, it was difficult to see the true color of the brown water, difficult also to see the disgusting things unabashedly floating on the surface, things like rusty beer cans, plastic bags, used rubbers, occasional turds.

It was very romantic.

I went with Herb to his farm that night in his old muddy pick-up truck. It took three hours to get there; he had to stop a few times to fix something under the hood; I guessed he was just showing off his mechanical acumen.

I was there for three days when Herb bought me a horse, a ten year old black gelding.

"I was buyin' some new pigs today at the market, and since they were sellin' horses too, I told 'em to go on an' throw inna nice horse for a little extra," he said.

"Go on down the barn and take a look at 'im. He's nice alright."

I decided to stay for awhile.

I took a trip back to Baltimore to pack some clothes and find a temporary home for my pet monkey. Then back at the farm, I rode the horse every day, while Herb rode his tractors, doing whatever it was that pig farmers do. I cooked a lot of pork; I sauteed vegetables but Herb didn't like them crisp; he liked them mushy, the way his mother made them.

We drank a lot of whiskey, and smoked a lot of grass at night, and he always sang and played the guitar before we went to sleep. He wrote new songs in his head every day. There wasn't any TV. His brothers and cousins were always around; they worked the farm too.

Sometimes friends of mine would drive up on the weekends from Baltimore. On these evenings with friends, while the biggest stars in the darkest skies spread out over us, Herb would take us for rides in the shovel tractor. In the dark we would all pile in the shovel and he would drive. He'd thunder across the land with us bouncing around and singing country hits.

I adopted one of the little piglets for a pet and brought him inside. He was so cute. Herb told me they were easily housebroken.

"Smart as whips," he said and he was right. Pigs make good house pets. The pig would always scratch with his cloven hooves at the door whenever he wanted to go out or come back in.

The house was huge, and cold, with no central heat. The main room was built a hundred and fifty years ago, and the rest of it was added on at the turn of this century. It hadn't been dusted or vacuumed in seventy years, so the dog and pig hair was so thick on the worn carpets that footsteps left impressions. All the furniture, the heavy drapes and the carpets that were probably vibrant seventy years ago were now the color of dried blood. Everything was monochromatic, the house and its' interior, Herb's clothes, the dirt on the boots. Even the stove and refrigerator, which were probably white at one time, were so caked with grease and pork blood that they were dark brown too. Despite this, the place didn't look dirty, for some reason; it just looked earthy. I liked it. His parents didn't. They lived in a modern trailer home down the road.

I lived there for four months and liked being the farmer's girl. I rode my horse back and forth across the land everyday, and got to know every acre... so when Herb was arrested for growing marijuana I couldn't believe it.

Where were those hidden acres? How had the police known about it?

I never did find out, but I saw pictures of the pot crop when I was taken in for questioning. In one color snapshot there was a fat cop standing beside a seven foot tall marijuana plant. He was posing like a proud fisherman with his giant dead fish strung up beside him.

The police tried to implicate me, but I was so obviously naive about the whole thing they let me go.

The worst part about it was Herb's father's reaction. He wouldn't bail him out.

On his own, Herb had no money... didn't even have a bank.

I tried to get the money together myself but I didn't know anybody who had 25,000 dollars. At the time I didn't even know anybody who had 25 dollars in one lump.

I stayed on at the farm without him for awhile, expecting that he'd be out any day, but the house became unbearable without him. I got very lonely. The pet pig got too big to keep indoors, so he ended as a regular pig. My horse disappeared, taken by the father or the brothers; I'll never know for sure.

I just sat on the red velvet sofa with the weak sunlight streaming through the muddy windows, my only companions the dust particles that floated around illuminated in the light. The trees became leafless; the ground turned hard with the first frost, so I went back to Baltimore and there found that even my monkey had died while I was gone.

I wrote Herb letters all the time but he never answered.

Finally I went to see him in prison.

He looked awful; his skin was sallow from being indoors; his blue eyes were empty; his hair was shaved.

I asked him why he hadn't answered any of my letters, and he said he couldn't read or write, and he was too embarrassed to ask any other prisoners to read him my letters because they were all busy reading constantly, and writing prison novels.

I had never known he was illiterate. I couldn't believe I hadn't known this.

So that's why all the books on the farm had been so dusty and upside-down on the shelves!

I read him my letters while I was there and I sent him a first grade English book. He had never gone to school, I found out, but that didn't make him stupid; he was one of the smartest people I've known.

What need did he have to go to school? His work was on the farm. What need did he have with the written word? He knew numbers; he was good at math; he could buy and sell pigs, and count them. He knew his relationship with the earth, and he knew all the carnal things, all the practical stuff.

He was born in that farm house on the same horse hair mattress that we slept on in the biggest bedroom. All his brothers had been born there, his father, his grandfather; in fact, his grandfather had died on it too.

"I'll probably die on this mattress," he once said when we were in bed together.

That day in prison he said something else. "I'm gonna die here in prison, Cookie. I feel my spirit ebbin' right outta me in this hell hole. It's a Godforsaken place, this here prison."

"You'll get out soon, Herb. Hold on, honey. You just need to be out in the fields again."

"Ain't never gonna be the same. Ain't never gonna be the same."

It was painful to see him with all that steel and concrete around him, the proverbial wild thing in a cage.

Bored of singing and playing his guitar, sick of the street-wise cellmates with their talk of thievery and guns and bars, tired of doing endless push-ups, he taught himself to read in prison, and soon he was writing ten page letters.

Grammar perfect, with spelling much better than mine, he finally found a way to write down the words to the songs he'd made up. He found out he'd been a poet all along, and found too, while consuming a book a day, that he was looking into a new world, and he responded to it like a man who'd been dying of thirst.

Eventually, after a year or two, I guess, I forgot what he looked like, the way he pitched hay, how he looked on a tractor, the way he sang. I stopped writing him letters and then he stopped writing me.

The next time I saw Herb was another year later at a Christmas party at my house. He'd just gotten out of prison, and he appeared all spiffy in his father's pre-

World War II blue suit with a little squirming black and white piglet under his arm. He offered it to me as a token of his love and then he asked me to marry him, right there in the doorway.

"Oh Herb... I... this... I... I can't... I'm really... sorry... I'm with somebody else now. I tried to write and tell you this... but ..."

"Who is this person you're living with?" He looked around, crushed.

I didn't recognize Herb at all. Who was this strange person on my doorstep? Everything had changed so much for me; things had been rushing in lightening speed. I'd totally forgotten about Herb. For him it was still two years ago, even though he was a different person, well read, well spoken, now on his way to becoming a very cultured person. Things had stood still for him.

I was the last woman he had seen. He probably jerked off thinking about me every night.

I felt guilty about that. I should have sent him some porno magazines, or found him a penpal, or something.

"Who's this person? I'd like to congratulate him," he said. The pig began to squeal. "Can I put this baby down?"

I nodded. The piglet trotted under the kitchen table. I started crying.

"He's over there," I said and pointed to the rock and roll hedonist I'd been living with. He was one of those romantic slow poison types, very drunk at the moment, sitting on the sofa drinking gin from the bottle, talking to another drunk. He was very different than Herb.

Herb walked over to him. "Hi. I'm Herb Eickerman, maybe your wife told you about me."

"She's not my wife," my drunk said, "but yeah, she told me. You out of prison? Just in time for Christmas. Have a drink."

He handed Herb the bottle, but Herb didn't take it. "You want a glass or something?"

"Don't you know that heavy drinking is slow death?" Herb said to him.

"Yeah. But who's in a hurry?"

"I see darkness all around that man," Herb said.

I guessed that he was talking about auras.

I looked over at my rock and roller. He was sitting in dim candlelight, wearing all black clothes, had dark green eyes, black hair and a three day five o'clock shadow on his face.

No wonder he looked shady.

"Look, Cookie, I don't feel much like partying," Herb said. "Have a nice life, and you can keep the pig. Do what you want with him. Eat him, whatever."

"I'd never ..." I started to say I'd never eat him but he stopped me.

"I found Jesus while I was in jail. He's going to keep me company." And he walked out.

My boyfriend, that prince of darkness, came to the door to stand next to me.

"You wanted to be with him?" he asked, "I'll leave. Don't worry about me. I'll just jump off a bridge or something."

"No, you don't have to do that," I laughed. "Just get me a drink."

He handed me the bottle.

Years later when the rock and roller had long moved out, and the piglet pet got too big to be a pet, I heard that Herb had married a redhaired Born Again Christian, and they were having little boy babies on the horse hair mattress.

Horse hair mattresses make a lot of noise, but they never lose their shape.

Route 95 South — Baltimore to Orlando

I don't remember why I went to Orlando with Lee. I guess I went because I needed some sun and there was a great place to stay. According to Lee, his brother's place was a mansion with a pool and gardens full of gladiolus and hibiscus flowers, grapefruit and orange trees.

"And we'll have fun. He has lots of cocaine," Lee said.

It was dark when we left for the trip. We walked in the bitter cold across a glass-strewn parking lot; the pieces of broken bottles glittering in the orange crime prevention lights made it look like a huge field of fool's gold. The cyclone fence we scaled had garbage and a lone ripped brassiere plastered to it in the stiff wind.

Approaching the highway, I realized that none of the cars would ever be able to see us in the dark with our black clothes on. I was right, we were there for about an hour with no luck at getting a ride.

Lee, who didn't possess the appropriate negativism wouldn't give up and go home. He just kept putting that

Johnny Walker Red to his lips while chanting Hare Krishnas.

"I chant to get rides," he said. "It works."

"Doesn't seem to be helping much tonight," I said.

"Wait. Be patient," he coaxed.

Another hour went by and we hadn't gotten a ride. I decided finally that he should hide behind the cement arch of the overpass and I would stand alone and hitchhike for awhile. It was the standard trick.

Sure enough a car stopped. I opened the door of the blue Ford and was a little disappointed to see that this person wouldn't do at all. He wore one of those psycho-sexual-disorder smiles. I closed the door.

Lee, as mad as I'd ever seen him, couldn't believe I turned the guy down.

"I'd protect you," he said with his hands on his hips.

"You'd fall asleep."

"No. I would have sat in the middle," he said.

"He would have raped you too. I'm a good judge of deviates. He was one all right," and that was that.

Before Lee got back to his hiding place, a Mercedes stopped and I opened the door. The driver looked okay. He was skinny with highly lacquered blond hair, a full mouth of good teeth, very clean manicured bejeweled hands. Here was a male version of a nouveau-riche hillbilly Farrah Fawcett, way before her time. Jascha Heifetz was blaring on the tape cassette.

Lee and I got in. He said his name was Cleo. He was going to Arlington, Virginia, right outside of Washington, DC.

"I'm on a lot of amphetamines," he said. I fell asleep.

When I woke up the car was parked in front of a large brick colonial house tastefully covered in English ivy. I was alone. I wondered what was going on.

Cleo and Lee soon appeared from the back of the house with a stereo, a color TV, silverware and a metal box.

"What's going on?" I asked as they loaded up the car.

"I just had to stop here and pick up a couple of things," Cleo said and smiled.

We left his house but fifteen minutes later we were parked in front of another large Tudor style house. Cleo was picking up a few things there too.

By the time we got to the fourth house the back seat was piled with ultra-modern state of the art appliances: Mister Coffees, La Machines, high performance vacuum cleaners, Kenmore toaster ovens. They also hadn't forgotten various valuable objets d'art, a few loose bottles of Korbel Brut... you name it. I figured out that I was an accomplice to Breaking and Entering and Grand Larceny so I thought it would be best to get out at the next Howard Johnson.

I found my bag under all the stuff and noticed a little gold statue of Pan lying on the floor with a Maxfield

Parrish print and a crystal jar of jelly beans. I liked that statue. Maybe I should ask Cleo for it. Oh, but why? He stole it anyway, so I put it in my bag without Cleo noticing. He had his back to me, driving.

"Take it," he said.

"I'm sorry. It was like impulse shopping. I can't believe you saw me do that." I handed it back to him.

"You can't hoodwink a hoodwinker," he said and winked at me in the rearview mirror. "It's yours. Take it."

I decided I wouldn't get out after all so we drove all the way with him until his turn off in Arlington.

He left us on the highway, after giving Lee a gas chain saw and his calling card. It had only his name and his phone number in lavender baroque script.

We got a ride by hanging out at a Howard Johnson and intimidating an old lady in pink foam curlers at the wheel of a grey Dodge. She was nervous; she didn't really want to pick us up at all.

"Oh, I understand totally," I said, "you don't really know us or anything."

She was leery of the chainsaw, she kept asking why we were carrying it. (Years later when I saw the film *The Texas Chainsaw Massacre*, I thought about this lady.)

When she dropped us off later Lee gave her the chainsaw as a gift and she was really happy. She'd always wanted one, she said.

The next ride was with a person in an Impala. Lee fell asleep in the back seat. This guy had something wrong with his neck. Big growths or something. He started talking about how he was turned away from the army induction center because of the varicosity in his scrotum and did I want to feel it? "Why don't you pull right over here on the shoulder?" I knew he would think I was going to take him up on the scrotum thing. When the car came to a stop I jumped out and yelled at Lee, "Time to go, Lee. This guy is 4F."

By this time we were in West Virginia and we got a ride with some mountain hippie types joy-riding with marijuana, seconals and beer. We got stopped by the cops and had to help swallow the grass and the seconals so they wouldn't get arrested. It was the least we could do in exchange for the ride.

By the time the seconals hit we were in another car speeding as the sky changed into pale blue. The Cuban guy driving the car told me there was a Spanish word for this time of the day.

"Madrugada," he said. "There's no equivalent in English."

I asked him if it included in its meaning the horrible way one feels after being awake all night. My bones felt hollow.

Before the sun had come all the way up, and the headlights were still on, we ran over a rabbit. Right before we hit him the rabbit froze; I guess he was paralyzed by the lights. I looked right into his eyes and saw his final instant of panic. I felt sick. We didn't say anything to each other, but the driver just pulled over and let us out. I guess he was superstitious.

We were both so tired now that we decided to rest in the woods for awhile but we crossed a little shallow swamp to get there and came out with leeches all over our ankles. The only way to get them off if you don't happen to be carrying kerosene was to piss on them. It wasn't easy; we must have stood there for forty five minutes thinking of running water.

Back out on the highway, we got a ride with a couple going as far as Sarasota. That was great.

When we got to the bottom of Georgia, Lee smoked a joint he'd gotten from the mountain hippies. Then he started throwing the *I Ching* coins. I ignored him. After that, while the woman in the front seat was trying to sleep, Lee started playing his harmonica. Music was not his forte but he thought it was, so when the couple asked him four times to stop playing, he argued the point until the couple dumped us out at three in the morning on a section of the highway that ran directly through the Okefenokee Swamp.

There was no moon. The sky was like black cotton batting that enveloped us in a way that felt like walking through clear water in a pool painted black. Very clear and cloudless was the night sky, so it was thick with stars. We even saw clusters of the dust from exploded supernovas deep in space, thousands of light years away.

All around was a nocturnal cacophony; alligators roared, lemurs, birds, and weird insects were yelling at each other. We kept walking and walking, blindly in the dark, along the deserted road that we couldn't see underfoot. There were no points of horizon, no beginning, no end to the highway; if the stars hadn't been there we would have no constellations to lead us; we would have fallen off into the swamp's mouth that gaped at us on each side. In all this blackness, it occurred to me that vicious reptiles and angry mammals might be rearing up for attack; hybrid swamp snake-rats could start licking at our heels at any minute.

Way back in the swamp were dim lights, probably the bunson burners of alligator wrestlers.

Lee played the harmonica until I grabbed it from him and tossed it into the darkness at the side of the road. It made a little splash as it hit the swamp water and all the animal sounds stopped for a moment.

We kept walking for hours until finally a black man in a dark pickup truck stopped for us. We could hardly see him.

He told us he was going to Orlando. Perfect! He was cracking something in his hand and eating it, and offered us some of whatever it was from a paper bag that was audible but not visible. I reached in. Oval things. Nuts!

"Pecans!" I said. I was hungry.

"I'ze haulin' a load obbem," he said, "Y'all take da hol bag."

"Thanks." Then we were all cracking and eating, rumbling along in the slow pickup. When the sun rose, there was silver and gold and every shade of tree laden with dew, all over the place. Willow, cypress, oak, and cottonwood trees were dripping with Spanish moss; the land was lush, fluffy. The air was sweet and warm. A flock of noisy Scarlet Tanagers and Cardinals lit up a cherry tree. The cicadas started droning. A pink Cadillac convertible with a pink woman driving whizzed by in the opposite direction. There were never any other cars.

The black man, who in daylight seemed like a cute smiling pocket gopher, pulled off the road and stopped next to a little orange shack with fatback cooking smoke coming from a grey pipe in the roof. There was a cardboard sign with the scrawled words "Brekfas 25 cent" taped with band-aids to the screen door.

"Les hav us som grits an aggs. And waatillya taaz dis heer coffee heer. Hmm hmm, ez good heer." He hopped out of the pickup.

"I'm buyin'," I said as the screen door slammed

behind us. The place was humming with black farmers in scrubbed overalls, little girls the color of buckwheat honey with hundreds of plastic barrettes in their hair, and their mothers in thin cotton dresses and flip flops. I don't think I've ever had a better breakfast in my life.

When we got to Orlando, the black man let us off not far from Lee's brother's house. It was regular suburbia. What a letdown. Lee's brother's house was not a mansion. It was more like a dilapidated pre-fab fake rancher. The place was overrun with weeds and the pool hadn't been cleaned in a long time; it was frothing green and slimy, with a thick surface layer of insect corpses riding on the little waves.

There wasn't much inside the house either except a TV set, a lava lamp and a few pieces of furniture covered with plastic. In the kitchen there were huge palmetto bugs and lizards scattering over the crusty dishes in the sink. The oranges and grapefruits were rotting on the ground, the flowers were all dried up and brown, and he hadn't seen any cocaine in a year.

The next day I took the golden Pan statue to an antique dealer and he gave me enough money to buy an airplane ticket back to Baltimore.

Next to me on the plane was a stranger who was putting out lines of cocaine on the little tray tables on the seat backs.

"Do this as we lift off. It's a rush," he said as he handed me a rolled up fifty dollar bill to snort with.

I thought about Lee and his brother doing nothing by the light of the lava lamp... well, maybe they were chanting and throwing *I Ching* coins on the stained wall to wall carpeting.

Far below was Highway 95 looking like an aluminum arrow with sparkling specks—cars. The distance Lee and I covered in three slow days would now take three quick hours. I turned to the generous person next to me and suddenly he didn't seem like a stranger after all.

Abduction & Rape — Highway 31 — 1969

"They were just three sluts looking for sex on the highway," the two abductors and rapists said later when asked to describe us.

This wasn't the way we saw it.

A lot of other people didn't see it this way either, but these were women. Most men who know the facts say we were asking for it.

Obviously you can't trust every man's opinion when it comes to topics like rape. A lot of honest men admit that they fantasize about it and that's healthy but the ones that do it to strangers, unasked, ought to have hot pokers rammed up their wee wees.

The worst part is there's no flattery involved in rape; I mean, it doesn't much matter what the females look like; it doesn't even seem to matter either if they have four legs instead of two. Dairy farmers have raped their cows even.

"It's great to fuck a cow," they say, "you can fit everything in… the balls… everything."

So I guess it just depends on your genital plumbing as to how you see the following story.

True, we were hitchhiking. True, we were in horny redneck territory, but we hadn't given it a thought.

It was a sunny day in early June, and Mink, Susan and I were on our way to Cape Cod from Baltimore to visit John Waters who had just finished directing us in his film *Multiple Maniacs*.

When we told him we were going to thumb it, he said incredulously, "You three?? You're crazy! Don't do it."

"He's just overly paranoid," I told Susan and Mink. "Hitchhiking's a breeze."

It made sense anyway because we only had about fifty dollars between us and above all we needed a beach.

Mink the redhead was dressed casually as always in a black leather jacket with chains, black fingernail polish and and tight black Levis. Susan, the brunette, was dressed as was her normal wont, in a daytime low cut evening gown, and I, the blond, was dressed conservatively in a see-through micro-mini dress and black velvet jacket.

This was not unusual for us, in fact benign, but in Baltimore at this time, the height of fashion was something like lime green vinyl pants suits, or other petroleum-based togs in chartreuse plaid or paisley that melted when the temperature was above 98.6. These clothes became one with Naugahyde car seats on a hot day. So people stared at us. They laughed right in our faces when they saw us.

"I hate to tell ya this," somebody would always take us aside, "but this ain't Hallor-ween."

To this day I can't figure out why we looked so odd to them. What did they see when they looked at their own outfits in their full-length mirrors?

In Susan's thrift store Victorian mirror that was about as useful as looking into a huge silver wrapped stick of Wrigley's, we put on our Maybelline black eyeliner lines and mascara, and were looking much better than any of the other displaced hillybilly beau monde on South Broadway that day.

"FINE MAKEUP, SENSIBLY PRICED" the Maybelline ad on TV said. I thought to myself how true it was. Couldn't beat it for a long trip; water-proof, smudge-proof, it sure held up.

For the twelve hour trip, we didn't forget our two quarts of Jack Daniels and a handful of Dexadrine Spantuals (they were new on the pharmaceutical market), and twenty Black Beauties. Aside from these necessities we had a couple of duffle bags of Salvation Army and St. Vincent de Paul formals and uniwear. We were all set.

On the street, we had no problem getting a ride due north.

The trouble started after about an hour into the journey. We had been travelling in an old green

Plymouth with a salesman and his *Gideon Bible*. He had run off the road into an embankment. Trying to follow our conversation, he'd gotten too drunk on the Jack Daniels, so we left him after he passed out behind the wheel.

"I don't think he was ready for us," Susan said, as we tumbled out of his car laughing.

"Let's make sure the next ride is going to Delaware or Connecticut," Mink suggested, "or at least a little further north."

We had no idea that we were standing smack in the middle of a famous love zone, Elkton, Maryland, the quickie honeymoon and divorce capital of the eastern seaboard.

Men whose eye pupils were dilated with goatish desire stopped before we could even free our thumbs. We decided to be selective. Apparently we weren't selective enough.

After a long dull lull in traffic, we hopped right into the back of a burgundy Mach 4 Mustang with two sickos, gigantic honkies, hopped up and horny on a local joy ride. They told us they were going to New York City, the Big Apple, they said.

It is a fact that retarded people do not know they are retarded; they just know that some people do not talk about stuff that interests them.

The conversation we were having in the back was beyond their ken; after a quart of liquor and five Black

Beauties apiece, we were a bit hard to follow, even for people who read all the classics.

I suppose they got jealous. They decided to get our attention by going around in circles, north, then south, then north again, passing the same toll booth four times.

Mink, the most astute of us, realized that her instinctive internal migratory compass was awry.

"We're trying to go north," she reminded them.

They just laughed.

"We see that you're playing some kind of circling game with your car." She was trying to make herself heard over the din of some backwoods hard rock bubblegum music that was blaring on the radio.

"Yeah, guys, I saw this same cheesey truck stop whiz by twice already," Susan pointed to a roadside diner that was whizzing by for the fourth time.

"I think they're just trying to get our attention," I said, taking the psychological angle.

"No," said Mink, "these guys are assholes. They're wasting our road time."

She should not have said that, but Mink has never been afraid of telling people about their personality flaws.

"Assholes, huh?" the driver scoffed, and he veered the car right off the highway and into a field of baby green beans and then got back on the blacktop and headed north again. The tires squealed the way they hardly ever do in real life, only in squalid car chase movies.

"Round dees parts we don't call nobody assholes," he said. "That's kinda impolite. We call 'em heiny holes." And they laughed and laughed.

"Well at least we're going north again," I said and in the very moment I said it I realized that it was a ridiculous thing to say.

There comes a time when even the most optimistic people, like myself, realize that life among certain humans cannot be easy, that sometimes it is unmanageable and low down, that all people are quixotic, and haunted, and burdened and there's just no way to lift their load for them. With this in mind I wanted to say something to Mink and Susan about not antagonizing these sad slobs, but right then the driver turned to me.

"You ain't going north, honey, you ain't going nowhere but where we're taking you."

These were those certain humans.

"Let's ditch these creeps," Susan said.

"We're getting out at the next truck stop," said Mink and she gathered her duffle bag like a career woman in a taxi with her attache case.

"Shut the fuck up," the driver said as a Monarch butterfly was creamed on his windshield. The wings mushed into his wipers as the blades squeaked over the splattered glass.

"Fucking butterfly guts," he said.

"We have knives," the guy riding shotgun said and he grinned at us with teeth that had brown moss growing near the gums.

"Big fuckin' deal," said Susan, "so do I," and she whipped out a buck knife that was the size of my mini skirt.

The driver casually leaned over and produced a shot gun and Susan threw the knife out the window.

Suddenly the effects of the Jack Daniels were wearing thin and the black reality of a speed crash was barreling in.

Mink began scribbling a note on a Tampax paper, "HELP!!! WE ARE BEING ABDUCTED BY ASSHOLES!!! CALL THE POLICE IMMEDIATELY!!!"

It was a note for the woman at the toll booth.

When we stopped there Mink started screaming and threw it at the woman. The note fluttered back into the car as we sped away.

"Have you ever fucked calves' liver?" Mossy Teeth said.

"How the hell ya supposed to fuck calves' liver?" the driver asked.

"Well, ya buy some fresh liver and ya put it in a jar and ya fuck it. It's better than a pussy."

Now that's disgusting, I thought, almost as disgusting as the popular practice in 17th century

France when men took live ducks and placed the heads of the ducks in a bureau drawer, put their dicks in the ducks and then slammed the drawer shut at the moment of their (not the duck's) orgasm. Men will fuck anything.

I suppose they also cooked the duck and ate it too.

They pulled into this long driveway. The dust was rising and matting the mucous membranes of our noses. Everybody sneezed.

I began to realize that for them we were party girls, that this wasn't something unusual, that girls around these parts were game for a good time, a gang bang, and that threats of murder might just be considered all part of the fun.

We bounced full speed down this backroad for quite awhile, passing vast stretches of young corn plants rustling and reflecting the sun on their new green leaves. I remember getting sliced by young corn plant leaves once, the same kind of painful wounds as paper cuts.

Mink and Susan and I couldn't even look at each other; our eyes hurt.

A white clapboard house came up near diseased elm trees in the distance. Some chickens ran away from the fenders. A rusted out pickup truck was growing weeds and a blue Chevy was sitting on four cinder blocks right next to a display of greasy old auto parts and an old gray dog that was trying to bark. We pulled up right to the house and from the front door, screen door slamming, came a big acne scarred man in his BVD underwear, a plaid flannel shirt with a sawed off shotgun.

"I told you once before, Merle, get off my property," the man hollered, "I'll blow your fuckin' heads right off your shoulders."

"My cousin's a little crazy," the driver said to us and he laughed.

"You wouldn't do no such thing," he bellowed to his cousin with the yellowish drawers on.

"Oh yes I would," the cousin said and aimed his gun at the windshield.

"You think he'd shoot us, El?" the driver asked his buddy.

"Sheet," the other one said, "he'd shoot his granny."

The screen door slammed again and then next to the cousin was a woman with dirty blond hair and dirty bare feet. She was wearing blue jean cut offs and a tee shirt that said MARLBORO COUNTRY on it. She looked forty-five but she was probably twenty.

A toddler of about two came to the door, pushed it, and fell out into the dirt. The baby started crying but nobody in the yard noticed. The baby got to his feet and stopped crying when he picked up a piece of car tire and put it in his mouth. He was teething, I guessed.

The woman grabbed the shotgun nuzzle. "Put that fucking gun down, Henry," she said.

"Leave goa dis gun, woman," Henry said and shook her off, aimed again. She jumped for it again, and in this moment the three of us, Mink, Susan and I started diving out of the car windows. Mink and Susan got out but Mossy Teeth, El, grabbed my thigh and held me fast. Merle spun the car around and we took off, making corn dirt dust in all the faces of everyone who was standing there in front of the house.

Susan and Mink tried to run after the car, yelling to me to jump. I couldn't now. It was too late. We were burning rubber up the gravel path while Merle and Ed were pulling me back into the car. They got me in the front seat with them. I was straddling the bucket seats.

I wondered what was going to happen to Mink and Susan, but I bet they wondered more what was going to happen to me.

What happened was this: I began to feel the mood change. As they were talking to each other I noticed that they sounded scared; El even wanted to get out and go home.

After a lot of fighting, Merle finally did let El go. He let him out at a backwoods package store.

Now Merle and his little brain began to wonder what to do with me. His buddy was gone. Who would fuel the fire?

I assumed that he would rape me. He wouldn't let me get away without that at least. Of course I didn't want to get raped, so I began to think of a plan.

I have always been an astute observer of sexy women and unsexy women, and in all my years I've never seen a crazy woman get chased by a man. Look at bag ladies on the street. They rarely get raped, I surmised. And look at burnt-out LSD girls. No men bothered with them much. So I decided that I would simply act crazy. I would turn the tables. I would scare him.

I started making the sounds of tape recorded words running backwards at high speed. This shocked him a bit, but he kept driving further into the woods, as the sun was setting and the trees were closing in.

"What the fuck are you supposed to be doing?" he asked me nervously. "You a maniac or something?"

"I just escaped from a mental hospital," I told him and continued with the backward tape sounds, now sounding like alien UFO chatter.

I think he was believing me, anyway he pulled off into the bushes and unzipped his pants and pulled out his pitifully limp wiener. He tried to get it hard.

For a second I saw him debating about whether or not he should force me to give him a blow job.

"Ya devil woman, ya'd bite my dick off wouldn't ya?"

He tried to force his semi-hard pee-wee rod into me as he ripped my tights at the crotch. I just continued with the sounds of the backward tape as he fumbled with his loafing meat.

This infuriated him. "I'm going to ask Jesus to help me on this one. Come on, sweet Jesus, help me get a hard on. Come on."

He was very serious.

This struck me as deeply hilarious. Praying to the Lord for a hard on was asking for the ultimate Bible text rewrite.

Not waiting to see whose side the Lord was on, I pushed his wiener quickly aside and threw open the door and dove out into the darkness. I ran faster than I'd ever run and I wasn't a bad runner.

As my eyes grew accustomed to the half-moon light, I saw that I was running into very deep woods. Aggressive brambles grabbed at my thighs, poison ivy licked at my ankles and yearling trees slapped me in the face.

After a long time I decided to stop running, so I got under a bush next to a pile of rocks. I felt a bunch of furry things scuttle away. Rats, or possums or raccoons, I guessed.

I laid there for awhile trying to see things in the darkness. And then I heard his voice.

He was far in the distance yelling, "Girl! Girl! Where the hell are ya?"

Did he think I was really going to answer?

As he got a little closer I saw that he had a flashlight and I got scared again. If his light found me there would be no hope. My white skin was very bright in the bluish flood of the half moon.

I had a black velvet jacket on with a black lining, so I ripped out the lining in two pieces and wrapped one around my head and the other on my almost bare legs. Those brambles had shredded my stockings.

No light would bounce off me now.

I was awake for a long time and then I just fell asleep, sure that he had given up the search.

At sunrise, or thereabout, I woke up. I didn't even have a hangover.

I felt very proud that I had melted so well into the underbrush, just like Bambi.

Without too much trouble I found this little dirt road and I started walking to the right.

"All roads lead to Rome," I told myself.

I guess I was walking for almost an hour when I heard a vehicle rumbling up behind me. For a second I thought maybe I better dive back into the woods, maybe it was Merle again but I turned and saw it was a little country school bus, a sixteen seater, a miniature version of the long yellow city buses. I stood in the middle of the road and waved it to a stop.

A woman was driving the bus and there was a load full of kids. I stood in the front of the bus and whispered my predicament; I didn't want to alarm the kids. She drove me to a ranger station and the ranger's wife gave me a cup of Lipton's.

I told my story and they were really peaceful sympathetic people. The ranger called the police station and I found out that Mink and Susan were there.

The ranger's wife liked me, I could tell, and they both drove me to the police station.

When they let me off the wife kissed me and said, "I hope everything goes well for ya, honey. That's a nasty thing ta happen. Watch yasself round these parts, there's some hanky panky round every corner here abouts. I know. My husband deals with it everday."

They drove off. I liked her.

Inside the police station the police weren't so nice, but they were patient with my story. They knew the guy. It was a small town.

"He was just released from Jessup's Cut," they said. "He's a bad ass for sure, always in trouble."

"His daddy's a religious man, though, had one hell of a religious upbringin'," one of them said.

Don't I knew it, I thought. He believed the Lord would raise the dead even.

It was good to be reunited with Mink and Susan. They told me that they were beside themselves with worry until about ten o'clock. That was about the time I was finally relaxing in the bush, I told them.

The police brought Merle in for questioning. They wanted to hold a kangaroo court right there in the next building. The law is quick in Elkton, Maryland.

In the courtroom I didn't press charges. That would mean lawyers and coming back there and a whole long drawn-out scene. I would lose anyway. I just wanted to leave that town as quickly as possible; anyway Merle was going back to jail for a false insurance claim, or something like that.

The cops then drove us to the bus station and told us that they better not ever see us on a highway again.

While we were waiting for the bus we decided to go to Washington, D.C., to the airport where we could maybe hitchhike a ride on a plane.

"Let's go in style, " I said. "No more cheap highways."

At the airport bar we met a marine biologist who was working in Woods Hole, Massachusetts.

"I'm flying back to work. I'm working with endangered bass," he said. "But my buddy's flying right into the P-town airport. He'll take you there. No problem. He should be landing here in about twenty minutes."

In mid-air we told them the story. We laughed a lot.

His friend flew us right into Provincetown.

"Wow, what luck!" Susan said.

I didn't think it was luck. Innocent people are sometimes rewarded.

Anyway, after everything we'd been through, we deserved it.

Sailing

Roy was a nice Jewish boy from Long Island, an asthmatic manic depressive who was really fun when he wasn't suffering. He came to visit me in Provincetown and enthusiastically told me he had just invested in a sail boat. He was going to the Caribbean, leaving from New York the day after tomorrow. He was really excited.

"You're really lucky, Roy," I said. "I wish I was going."

"HEY! Maybe you can! You want to? Why not? Yeah. You know how to sail, right?"

"A little," I said.

"We need a cook. You want to go?"

I didn't even think about it. "Sure, yeah. I've never been to the Caribbean. Why not?"

"I don't know how to sail at all," he laughed, "but I guess this is the best way to learn. Right?"

He had bought the boat with two other guys, "veteran sailors," he assured me. It all sounded okay to me; as long as the other two knew more than I did about sailing everything ought to be fine. I packed some cruise wear and went with Roy the next day to Long Island where the boat was docked.

It was a forty-two foot sloop, made in the thirties, all teak wood, well cared for and seaworthy; resting in the water near Roy's house, it looked graceful and sophisticated with the waves licking its smart hull.

The other two proud boat owners were Tom, the red-haired alcoholic navigator and Jerry (I'll call him Jerry, because he looked and acted exactly like Jerry Lewis with a hangover at the end of a flop *March of Dimes Telethon*.) His real name I have mercifully forgotten.

The sun was sinking on the Long Island Sound when we shoved off, but it wasn't red; in fact, you couldn't even see it for all the ash-colored clouds moving in. That wasn't a good sign, but we left anyway.

By the time we passed between the shores of Queens and the Bronx it started to rain and the water was slapping up, spitting and splashing us in the faces in the dark. As we started rolling into the bottleneck of the Narrows, Jerry was having a hard time maneuvering around the big freighters. I couldn't figure out why the sails were still up, why we weren't using the engine. Considering all the rain and all the ships we were almost hitting, it just didn't make sense.

Roy got an asthma attack from fear, on top of being seasick. He should have gone up on deck for air but he couldn't bring himself to do that, so he was throwing up all over the cabin. He obviously wasn't cut out for sea travel; I think it was the first time he'd ever been on a boat. He kept saying he wanted terra firma.

While I was busy cleaning up after him, paper towels in hand, I happened to look up to the deck, starboard side and saw a ship so close that I was able to look right into one of its porthole windows and read 60 Watt on a bare light bulb that was hanging in there. The ship looked like a floating World Trade Center.

In my peripheral vision I noticed two other monster ships barreling portside, blowing their horns. Jerry did some amazing acrobatics at the wheel and we missed all three ships. It was just luck.

I was really angry and getting scared, so I climbed up on the deck and started inching my way out to the jib sail.

"What the hell are you doing?" Jerry screamed at me.

"I'm taking down the jib sail and you're going to take down the main sail and turn on the motor. We're going to die out here if you don't," I screamed at him with a mouthful of sea water. Swells were hitting me from all sides.

"The motor doesn't work," he screamed back and a wave smacked him in the kidneys.

I was mortified. I didn't know what to say to this, so I went back to the galley. Did he think we were going to go all the way to Jamaica without a motor? That was insane.

In times of crises, on TV, someone always resorts to making coffee. Maybe coffee was the right thing at this moment. I tried to light the stove, but I wasn't too familiar with propane; I guess I opened the lever too far, so when we hit a dip in the wave, the propane leaked from the stove's face and it ignited the whole stove. The flames started licking the teak cabinets and I looked around for the fire extinguisher but I couldn't find it. I'd seen it somewhere... where?!? Nevermind, there wasn't time to look. With all the adrenaline strength I could muster I picked up the flaming two hundred pound stove and tossed it up to the deck. Tom and Jerry jumped back, but then they picked it up and threw it overboard. They must have burned their hands.

No one said a word.

Around midnight he put in at Sandy Hook, New Jersey and Jerry started screaming about the stove, how he'd paid so much money for it, how HE wasn't going to buy a new one; I had to buy a new one.

"It was all your fault!! Why the hell didn't you use the fire extinguisher?"

"I couldn't find the fire extinguisher!" I screamed back at him.

"Look. It's right here. Right here." He looked around

and couldn't find it either. "Well, it was here." He found it laying on his bed in his cabin room.

"Good place for it," I said.

"Who put this in here?!?" he demanded. Nobody answered.

Through all this, Tom the navigator was drinking rum, not saying a word, just fixing the engine, covered in black grease. Roy was packing his bag. He still looked green.

"I'm getting off here. I don't think I'm cut out to be a sailor. I'll meet you in Jamaica. Call me when you get there, I'll fly down." He hopped on the dock. "Have a great time." He paused a moment, wondering why he felt unsteady, "God, I'm swaying. I must be really sick. I feel unsteady." He sat down on one of the pilings. "I'm going to see a doctor."

"Don't worry about that, Roy. What you're feeling now, every old salt feels when he jumps on land. Those are your sea legs," I told him and laughed. Roy did not think it was one bit funny. He was the classic hypochondriac.

"That wobbly feeling goes away in a little while," Tom said.

Roy took out his hankie and blew his nose, then he got up and wobbled away fast, down the dock and onto the shore, leaving me with these two strangers. I never ever saw Roy again. I wonder what happened to him.

We started out the next day at dawn. The engine was all fixed, but I found that the sloop couldn't take most of the inland waterways; it's main mast was fifty feet tall so most of the bridges were too low for us to fit under. Not only this, the boat drew six feet (it's underside ran six feet deep) and most of the waterways weren't deep enough. The inland waterways were for small craft, cabin cruisers and sail boats with more sensible proportions, so we had to travel along the coast in the open ocean and it was hurricane season. The three of us weren't so enthusiastic about the open ocean anymore; we wanted the easier route, the calm man-made canals of the inland waterways.

Every day the sky was mottled with black clouds, the sea was high, it looked fat and angry. People who've never travelled on the ocean have no idea how scary it is to be on a little boat out there with no land in sight, waves towering over you while you go into the valley of a swell with nothing to see except water... water and sky, no other boats anywhere, no semblance of any kind of firm reality at all. The main thing one shouldn't do is imagine things. One shouldn't think about the boat tipping over, just falling over and rolling under. Things like that happen all of a sudden. A gigantic three story high wave could whollop the boat broadside. Splash! Whoops! You're gone! No hint of a boat in about three minutes! If you don't get sucked under with it, then where are you?

I decided not to think about this aspect of ocean travel, so I opened my book, *Interviews with Film Directors*, and started reading aloud, trying to concentrate on how Alfred Hitchcock wanted to print the film *Vertigo* on latex instead of celluloid so he could stretch it and make audiences dizzy. I wanted to ask Jerry to head the boat toward earth but I didn't dare. He would have just gone further out to sea. He was still angry with me.

By dusk Jerry was heading toward shore and thank God, there was Atlantic City on the right. Far, far in the distance the ferris wheel was the size of a dime, but I swear the smell of hotdogs was reaching me when the wind blew in our direction. It was like the smell of the earth.

That night we put in around Atlantic City and Jerry yelled at me all night about the stove. Two days later after one night at Cape May, New Jersey, the sky broke, the sight of the sun made everything seem less scary in the open ocean; it was the first really bright day we had. We made it to the waters of Maryland.

In familiar waters, with the sun out, and Tom singing, and even Jerry in a good mood, I decided that I'd do some fishing.

That was a ridiculous idea.

Moving along at that speed, the baited hook was just trailing along the surface of the water way behind the boat. Fish couldn't even get a nibble.

A seagull started following us. After awhile he swooped down into the water, and when he flew back up into the sky, there was something obviously wrong with him. I noticed then he had my hook in his mouth, I had a bird like a kite on a string. This was horrible. He was screaming like a human being.

I didn't know what to do. I couldn't leave the hook in his mouth, I had to get him out, so I started to reel him in.

"Cut him loose," Tom suggested.

"Oh, I can't do that, he'll die."

"Let's get into that inlet there and get the hook out!" I pleaded with Jerry.

He was already heading there. Maybe Jerry was alright after all. Did he like birds? People who like birds can't be all bad.

In the Concoteague Inlet I reeled in the bird. He was all muscle, flapping and screeching; it wasn't easy. It was like fighting with a five hundred pound tuna. My arms were aching. Tom and Jerry wanted to help but I had to do this myself; I had to. When I finally got him aboard I put him under my arm. He bit and scratched me until my hands and arms were bleeding, but from his mouth where the hook was, he was bleeding worse. I was crying; the bird was whining, and it took forever, but I finally got the hook out and let him go. He flew away wailing and bleeding. I wondered if he'd die. He certainly wouldn't be able to eat for awhile.

This was too much, not a good sign. It all seemed too much like the Ancient Mariner with the albatross. I wanted to end the journey, pack my bags and leave. After everything else that had happened on this trip, I took this for an omen, a harbinger of further problems. Besides, it had taken five days to get from New York to Ocean City, Maryland. Definitely it was an outmoded way to travel. Too much for a modern girl.

"I have to say goodbye here, fellas," I said and I don't think they were too sorry to see me go. "Let me know where you are in the Caribbean and I'll try to send you some money for that stove."

"Never mind, Jerry can well afford to buy another stove. He's just too cheap." Tom spit out these words, like he'd been dying to say them for days. Jerry glared at him and said something like fuck you or up yours... something lame. They were still fighting as I walked the length of the pier and turned toward the town. The next person to jump ship would be Tom, I guessed. Then what would Jerry do?

I had gotten off the boat only forty miles from where my sister lived. That was handy. I called and told her I was on my way; then I hopped on a bus and was there in an hour.

"What took you so long?" she asked. "Long? That wasn't long. If I'd been sailing here, it would have taken two days."

The Birth of Max Mueller — September 25, 1971

The night Max was born mongrels roamed in packs. The moon had turned to blood and the hungry hounds were howling for it in wild lunar lust.

I was in pain in the maternity ward of the Hyannis Hospital, but this wasn't plain pain, no; this was the kind of pain that for reasons of sanity, the mind doesn't allow a woman to remember. It was relentless, unbearable, hideous, appalling, horrifying. I was undergoing internal gut ripping tubal wringing, organ stretching, muscle pummeling, bone cracking. I was the grand martyr. Prometheus knew no pain like this. Lamaze had lied.

I couldn't believe that women went through this to have children. After this why would anyone want to have another one?

In my hallucinations caused by pain delirium, I watched dozens of night birds throw themselves, screaming, against the glass of the windows... or was it just hail?

Every sound was magnified. Everything roared.

The fluorescent light was buzzing like a chainsaw, the

clock ticking on the wall was Chinese water torture, the cries from other women in the next rooms were as earsplitting as the wrong songs of distressed Humpback whales. The white tiles on the floor were so clean they were whistling. Even the usually silent plants on the window sill, benevolently doing their miraculous carbon monoxide to oxygen exchange, were wheezing with asthmatic photosynthesis.

From my antiseptic bed with the stiff flash-pasteurized sheets in a severely blank hospital room I could see, though the window, the black sky and the Libra constellation of stars rising in fast motion. Other galactic nebuli and meteor dust were swirling backwards, the red moon was closing in, but maybe it was really a UFO with atomic power pack problems, reverse electromagnetic damage.

Was this happening?

I abandoned all hope. I was sinking into the bed; I was drowning; I was falling. I was being sawed in half like the woman in the box with the magician.

So… this was childbirth? Nobody told me about this part. This wasn't fair. Men didn't have to do this, but they couldn't ever deal with this anyway, men can't stand pain without snapping into idiocy or vegetable-dom.

"What the hell is the deal here?" I yelled at the nurse who walked in eating a ham and swiss on rye and reading *House and Garden*. Mayonnaise was on her weak chin.

"Just calm down, my dear. It'll all be over before you know it. It's not so bad." "Have you ever done this?" I asked. I needed real sympathy.

"Well, no... but I've seen it thousands of times." The mayonnaise on her chin must have been imitation mayonnaise, because it wasn't melting into her pores. It was just sitting there, getting on my nerves.

"If you've never done this you don't know anything about it. Why don't they hire some nurses around here who can be sympathetic? Some nurses who've had children?" I hissed.

"Why don't you try your Lamaze breathing again?"

I was incredulous. I just gaped at her.

"THE LAMAZE METHOD! Are you kidding?!? Don't you think I've already tried that?" At this point the Lamaze Method was about as useful as sandals in a blizzard.

She just looked me over with eyes very dead. Shark attack victims have described shark's eyes that looked like this.

I wanted to escape. I decided to get to the window and jump out to die to end the pain, but the nurse wouldn't let me.

"Lie down," she said, "just lie down."

"This isn't a natural position for childbirth... lying down... I want to squat. Why can't I squat?"

"We can't let you squat."

"This is really stupid. All I want to do is squat. Women in Africa dig a hole in the ground and squat over it when they're giving birth. The baby comes right out."

"Look, do you want pain medication?" she asked like a heroin dealer, smiling. I remembered that line about the first one being free, which isn't true in real life.

"No. I'm a martyr," I screamed, "can't you see that?" I was not a martyr; I was delirious. I had quit drugs and alcohol for the whole nine months of pregnancy; I hadn't even taken an aspirin; why take something on the last day?

I tried to sit up, roll over, squat, stand in bed, turn, thrash, but she kept holding me down.

"We're going to have to restrain you if you keep trying to move around," she said.

"I can't believe this. What is this place? Dachau?" I screamed. I should have stayed home and had the baby. Friends of mine who had their babies at home were up and active until they felt the baby coming out. Then they just squatted in an easy chair and dropped the baby.

I was so angry I wanted to cry. I held the bridge of my nose the way Marlo Thomas did on the *That Girl* show when she was trying not to cry.

"I'm really thirsty. I haven't had any liquid for twenty four hours," I said. "Can you get me some water?"

"We can't let you have water. Just in case we have to

anesthetize you, we don't want anything in your stomach."

I knew all that. They didn't want me to get sick on the anesthesia, and throw up, and have the vomit caught in my esophagus. If only they knew; it took a lot more than a little anesthesia to make me puke.

"Jesus, I have to pee," I said. I did have to pee and while I was in the bathroom I could drink some water from the faucet.

She wouldn't even let me go to the bathroom.

"I have to pee," I screamed. "That's all. Just pee!"

"We can't let you get up," she said. "I'll get you a bed pan. Wait."

While she was out I got up, went to the bathroom and took a piss. I also put my parched lips on the faucet and sucked water, like a person who had been lost in the desert.

The nurse came back. She caught me while I was shuffling back from the bathroom. She was irate.

"I can't believe you got up when I told you NOT TO! Get back in bed and lay down!" She tossed the bedpan aside and handed me a weird oblong yellow thing on a lollipop stick. "This is the only thing you can have before an operation. It'll take your thirst away. Suck on it."

I did.

On this whole planet, there are not too many things eatable or suckable that I cannot easily recognize or give nomenclature to. This yellow thing was one of those things. It was a preoperative horror on a stick, but it was sweet, sort of, so I used it, and it did put some moisture on the tongue. I had been in labor for almost twenty-four hours and I was dry. Anything remotely wet was fine.

When the next contraction came, and the pain was even worse than before, I decided I was dying. Women die in childbirth all the time. I had to think of something else. I forced myself to relax.

Okay. If this was the way it was going to be, then it better be worth it. This kid had better be as formidable as the pain. This kid had better come out of the womb speaking quantum physics, or be telekinetic, or have white hair and purple eyes, or be able to levitate, or have a blue aura, or be the new messiah, or be clutching gold in his little fists, or at least speak like the dolphins speak.

A couple of hours later, he just came out. The head and the shoulders were a push, but the rest of the body just slipped out. It felt like a fish sliding out, like a bloated mackerel.

My baby was a boy and he looked like all the rest of the babies I had seen the day before in the nursery, red and shrivelled and screaming. The umbilical cord looked exactly like a gray coiled telephone wire.

The doctor looked him over. "It's a boy. OH!… but what's this?"

Naturally I panicked. "WHAT'S WRONG WITH HIM!?!"

"Oh... ahh... ahh, it's nothing. I'm sorry... I thought..." The doctor was laughing then. "It's just a birthmark, a black birthmark where he'll never see it in his life... under his scrotum."

There was nothing else weird about him except for his hair. He had the longest, blackest, thickest hair anyone had ever seen at that hospital. And he had a cowlick, ridiculously sticking straight up from nine months of amniotic hair setting. The nurses' aides all went wild about his head of hair. They gave him an Elvis Presley pompadour for his hospital photos. That was something worthwhile.

When the dad saw his son for the first time, he looked pleased, but he told me he was terrified.

I held my kid in my arms when they brought him to me to breast feed. He was like a little monkey, wirey and solid... no fat at all, with strong legs like a mature frog.

I drifted to sleep with him beside me.

"Goodnight, Max," I said to him, "I'm going to sleep now."

I had a dream that Max spoke to me. "It's a good idea to get lots of sleep now, while you have a chance," he suggested in baritone, "because for many years to come, you're going to need it."

I woke in horror. "I'd better get a Doctor Spock book," I told myself, then I fell asleep again. It was to be the last time I slept soundly for sixteen years.

Pink Flamingoes

"What's the worst thing that can happen to me when I eat the dog shit?" Divine asked us, while we were sitting around the set waiting for John Waters who was doing some exterior shots. Van Smith, the makeup man, was painting Divine's face. David Lockhary was arranging his blue hair and drinking coffee; Mink was putting her contact lenses in; Bonnie was reading the *Baltimore Sun*; I was trying to remember my lines.

There was no question that Divine would eat the dog shit. He was a professional. It was in his script, so he was going to do it.

"We'll find out what'll happen," I said.

It was a secret. Only a few people involved with *Pink Flamingoes* knew about the shit-eating-grin scene at the end of the film. John wanted to keep it quiet. Maybe he was afraid some other film maker might beat him to it, steal the shit-pioneer award. Anyway too much word of mouth, now, would deplete the surprise for the film-goer later.

"We'll talk to a doctor," Van said, pausing mid-stroke with the liquid eyeliner brush.

"I'll do it if it doesn't kill me," Divine said and laughed.

"Pretend it's chocolate," Bonnie suggested.

In the world there are many brave people: those who climb Mt. Everest, those who work in Kentucky coal mines, those who go into space as astronauts, those who dive for pearls. Few are as brave as actors who work with John Waters.

We didn't think he was asking too much. We didn't think he was crazy, just obsessed.

"Call a doctor right now," Mink said.

"Call a hospital. Call Johns Hopkins!" I said, and handed him the phone.

"Why belabor the situation? Why worry? Get it over with," said David.

"Dial the phone," said Mink.

"Call pediatrics. Tell them your son just ate dog shit. See what they say," Van suggested.

Divine started dialing the hospital and reached a doctor.

"My son just accidentally ate some dog feces," Divine said. "What's going to happen to him?"

"What's he saying?" Bonnie asked.

"Shh... " he said to Bonnie. "And then what?" Divine asked in the phone. "Hmmmhu, hmmmhu, OK, then. Thank you." He hung up.

"So?" asked David.

"He didn't sound too alarmed," Divine said. "I guess it's just a routine question for a doctor. He said all I have to be careful about is the white worm."

"What's that supposed to mean?" Mink asked.

"Tape worms," Divine said, "that doesn't sound too dangerous."

"You don't have to swallow it anyway," Van said.

"He said to check out the dog. Take it to a vet," Divine said.

"John is doing that," I said.

"What kind of dog is it?" Mink asked.

"A miniature poodle," said Divine.

It was suggested to John to do the take in two shots, first the dog does his duty, then cut. Replace the real shit with fake shit. Divine eats it. Cut. But John knew, we all knew, that audiences wouldn't fall for that.

"No. NO. Everybody would know we replaced the real shit for fake. Divine's gotta scoop it right up still warm off the street," John had said a few days ago.

This was show biz. Divine didn't balk and he wasn't the only one. Mink Stole was going to do a big scene that called for her red hair to catch on fire. The dialogue would be: "Liar, liar, your hair's on fire." She didn't seem afraid at all.

"I'll do it. There'll be fire extinguishers there."

"You could use a wig," I said.

"Somebody already suggested that to John. No. Audiences want the truth," Mink said.

The day John was about to shoot the hair-on-fire scene, he changed his mind; he decided it would be too dangerous after all. They tested a piece of Mink's hair and it just smoked and sizzled and smelled awful. There'd be no dramatic effect; it wouldn't have burst into flames. John was a little disappointed but he'd think of something else. Mostly when John came up with these kinds of ideas for his actors, he was testing us or half joking; the actors were the ones who took him seriously, we were the hams. Actors know scenes like these make stars.

"Aren't you supposed to do some scene where you get fucked by a chicken?" Divine asked me.

"Fucked by a real chicken?" Mink asked me.

"How?" asked Bonnie.

"In the script it says Crackers cuts off the head of a chicken and he fucks me with the stump," I said.

"Oh that sounds easy," Divine said.

"Yeah, that's easy compared with what you have to do," I said to Divine.

"Chickens scratch pretty bad," David said. Even without their heads."

"Bird wounds can be dangerous," Van said.

I thought about Hitchcock's *The Birds*, but those were seagulls and I knew just how powerful seagulls could be. Compared to them, chickens were jellyfish.

"I'm not worried about some little scratches," I said.

"But I don't think I can watch while the head's being cut off."

"Oh come on. Chickens don't know they're dying. They're not smart enough," David said.

There were a couple other scenes in the film we talked about.

"The whole trailer has to burn to the ground. That could get out of hand, couldn't it?" I asked.

"John's going to have a fire truck there," Van said.

"Doesn't Linda Olgeirson have to be artificially inseminated on camera? Down in the pit?" Mink asked.

"She'll have a stand-in," Bonnie said.

"It's a close-up beaver shot. Nobody will know it's not her. She doesn't want to expose her pussy for the audience. I wouldn't do that either," I said.

"No, I wouldn't either," said Mink.

We would all eat shit, catch on fire, fuck chickens, but we wouldn't do close-up crotch shots. There has to be a line drawn somewhere.

"I have to show my dick," David said.

"But you're going to have a turkey neck tied on it," Mink said. "That doesn't count."

"Elizabeth is going to expose her tits and her dick, David. So what are you complaining about?" Divine said, and we all agreed.

Making this film, we went to bed every night really excited for the next day's shoot. Perhaps there are other actors who can tell you that making films is really boring. This film wasn't. On big budget sets, actors go into their private trailers, waiting for their camera time. Not on this set. We were all in the same room between takes, busy changing costumes, remembering lines, bitching about bit actors stealing scenes, layering makeup, getting ready to emote. There were no private trailers around.

Making low budget films is work, but it's fun, it's more fun than working in big budget films. If you're an actor, there is nothing more rewarding, despite the meager pay. On small films you get to know the whole cast and crew in a day, and all of these people are much more inventive because of the limited budget; they create effects that wouldn't have been born if there was more money. Necessity is the mother of invention; this is true. John is a master at this, his imagination runneth over.

Before we started shooting *Pink Flamingoes*, I was living in Provincetown with two month old Max and Tom O'Connor, Max's step-father of the moment. Max and I were staying with my mother in the Baltimore suburbs for the duration of the filming, but it wasn't turning out well living there with Mom and Dad.

My mother knew there was filming going on, but I didn't tell her Max was one of the stars, cast as the newborn infant bought by a lesbian couple, and I certainly didn't tell her I was going to have to fuck a chicken.

"Let me read the script," she'd say all the time.

"Ah… well… I don't have the script here. I left it on the set."

"Then tell me about the movie. About your part," she'd say.

"Not much to tell. It's the story of two rival families. I play the intermediary, the spy," I said.

"What's the rivalry? Are they criminal families?" she asked.

"Not really, but sort of," I said. How in the world could I describe that film to my mother?

A few days later, when John came to pick up me and Max for the day's shoot, my mother stopped me from leaving.

"Where do you think you're going?" she demanded.

"I'm going to the set," I said.

"OH NO YOU'RE NOT," she screamed, "I FOUND THAT SCRIPT AND I READ IT AND YOU'RE NOT GOING ANYWHERE NEAR THAT SET!"

I sat down in the Victorian chair for a second. "Mom, it's not like you think. This movie's going to be funny. It's not porno. It's a whole other kind of film… it's art… it's…" I was at a loss for the right word, the label that would legitimize the film for her. How could she ever understand?

boarded horses were supposed to be ke̜
were too wild to feel comfortable in a barn
was a half-finished log cabin, and a two-story
with blue glass windows Vickie was buildin̖
herself.

There were lots of animals, a mean male goat tie̖
a plum tree, three mild-mannered milk goats, fou̖
horses, three cats, two dogs, an intelligent pig and very
dumb chickens.

I've known a few chickens in my time and they're all
really stupid, even though they lay perfectly good eggs.

The first couple of weeks I stayed there, my only
interest was riding the horses, except they were
practically uncatchable; they romped in their acreage of
fenced woody hillsides, hiding behind trees, galloping
away whenever they saw somebody coming with a
bridle and a pail of oats.

The only horse I could ever nab regularly was the
big brown gelding, Mory. He was fairly docile once
bridled, but had been hit by a Mack truck years before
so he was spooked. When anyone was on his back, he
always hallucinated obstacles in his path, so he would
leap suddenly to one side or the other with no warning,
throwing the unwary equestrian's fanny into the dirt.
Since there weren't any saddles it was always a test.

I once caught the smart young mare, who was fast
and hard to handle. She was an incredible ride; I had a

eat time until she threw me and came back to trot on ny stomach. I never thought I could lose interest in iorses so fast.

The night the house burned down, Tony and Laura were across the river at an all night party. Vickie had gone to Vancouver for the weekend on an antique buying spree. The house was full of the stuff. The guests, Don, Loo, Howard and myself were busy that evening with Don's cocaine and old photographs. Max was crying upstairs; he didn't want to go to sleep at all. Finally I brought him down with us. I was really angry at him.

When we ran out of cocaine and photographs, Don went out to his little Volkswagen to get more.

He wasn't gone for more than five seconds.

"THE ROOF... " he screamed. He was all choked up, his mouth was moving but he wasn't making any sounds. We thought maybe he was O.D.ing on cocaine or something. "FIRE... ROOF... THE HOUSE... IT'S ON FIRE!!!"

"What?" we all asked.

True, we had been getting warmer all along; we'd been shedding layers for a half an hour; we had all commented on it, but we thought it was the coke or the whiskey.

"THE TOP OF THE HOUSE IS ON FIRE!"

We threw back our chairs and ran out to see most of

the roof blazing. Max had been upstairs only an hour before.

"CALL THE FIRE DEPARTMENT!!!" I screamed. I picked up the receiver but it was dead. The phone lines on the roof must have burned already.

"DON'T THEY HAVE A FIRE EXTIN-GUISHER SOMEWHERE?" Loo shouted.

"DON'T KNOW!" Howard screamed.

"I SAW ONE IN THE BARN!" I yelled. The barn was so far away.

"SOMEBODY RUN AND GET IT!!" we all shouted and Loo made tracks.

"I THINK IT'S TOO LATE FOR A FIRE EXTINGUISHER!" Don sweated.

"LET'S GO UPSTAIRS AND THROW BLANKETS ON IT!" Howard took the stairs five at a time.

Behind him, Don and I couldn't go further than the top of the stairs. Instantly our eyeball retinas were singed, our eyelashes gone with the heat. By now all the rooms were roaring red and gold; it wasn't just flames; it was a massive inferno. There wasn't any need to say anything; we just tumbled down the stairs.

"LET'S SAVE WHAT WE CAN DOWNSTAIRS!" Howard looked around frantically.

I picked up Max and a bunch of coats that were hanging on the door. I ran out and untied the goat from the plum tree and tied Max to it. I ran back inside. Don and Howard were breaking windows and throwing valuables out. I picked up a huge antique gold-framed mirror, but I dropped it on the way and even the frame fell away, but I took one piece out anyway, then I ran back in. Everything was whizzing out the windows, chairs, books, pots, pans, vases, lamps, the stereo.

Howard and I hysterically grabbed a huge plastic container with a lid on it. We carried it out carefully, whatever it was; we would risk our lives saving it. Later we found out it was the garbage.

"GET THE COATS!" Don yelled.

"GET THE CATS!" Howard had breakables piled in his arms.

"CATS ARE OUT!" I remembered seeing all three of them huddled near the wood pile outside.

Loo came running in wincing from the sudden blast of heat on her face, "I COULDN'T FIND THE FIRE EXTINGUISHER, BUT I RAN TO THE LASSER'S AND CALLED THE FIRE DEPARTMENT!" The Lassers were the people who owned the farm way down the road.

"AND?" we asked.

"THEY SAID THEY'D COME BUT THERE WASN'T MUCH THEY COULD DO!"

"WHAT'S THAT SUPPOSED TO MEAN?"

"DON'T KNOW!" she said.

Don was gathering sleeping bags and silverware while Loo picked up some blankets and rugs and crystal stemware. Howard and I carried out the Victorian blue velvet couch, the hanging Tiffany lamp, a mahogany rocker, radio, clock, some food from the refrigerator, and three bottles of Canadian Five Star Rye whiskey.

After these trips we came back in and looked around like maniacs. We looked at the walls. All the paintings were hanging there waiting. We went into instant art panic. It was getting dangerously late to be in the house, the roof was about the fall.

"THIS ARTIST IS MORE FAMOUS!" Howard yanked a painting off the wall.

"BUT THIS ONE'S WORTH MORE!" I grabbed another. We hadn't much time.

"NO TAKE THIS ONE! IT'S OLDER!" Howard pulled one down.

"BUT LOOK AT THESE BRUSHSTROKES."

"NO! THIS ONE."

"GIMME THEM ALL. I'LL CARRY THEM ALL!" I realized it was completely ridiculous to be standing there fighting over art while the house was beginning to crumble in flames. I stacked as many as I could under my arm. Howard scooped up some more paintings and piled them on his back with the wires around his neck.

We decided it was to be the last trip back inside.

I went over to the plum tree where Max was roped. He was thirteen months old at the time, a toddler who wobbled away every chance he could. Toddlers know no danger; the minute you put one of them down they run off, right into anything, traffic, a deep pool, a canyon. If I hadn't tied him he would have toddled as fast as he could into the flames.

Right then he was as happy as a clam, pulling the ears of one of the cats and smiling at the bright orange fire.

I untied him and held him on my hip and we all looked at the house totally engulfed by flames. As I looked through the livingroom window, I saw Max's boots hanging on a nail on the mantelpiece. I'd put them there to dry before we'd had dinner, because he ran into the river earlier that day. My boots were there too. They got soaked when I ran after him. I looked at Max's feet. He was totally barefoot; so was I but I just hadn't noticed during the panic. It wouldn't do at all to be barefoot in November in the Canadian Rockies.

"Hold Max a minute," I said calmly to Loo and I attempted to walk back in through what was left of the front door.

"Where you going?" Howard grabbed me.

"I have to get Max's shoes."

"You can't go back in there." He looked at me like I was crazy.

"I have to. Max is barefoot." I released Howard's grip and started again, but Howard pushed me aside. He went back in himself, literally risking his life.

"HOWARD! NO! IT'S NOT YOUR RESPONSIBILITY!" I screamed at him, but he was already in there. We held our breath.

Howard did not lose his life, instead, he lost his eyelashes, eyebrows and a lot of his hair. He got Max's boots and mine too.

Then we just stood there watching it burn.

The fire department came eventually, but there wasn't anything they could do; there weren't any fire hydrants within twelve miles.

"Don't you people carry water on the fire engines?" Loo asked. They sort of laughed at this, but were actually very sympathetic.

They cut some wires and soon left.

We spread some blankets on the ground, opened a bottle of whiskey and sat watching the upstairs start to crumble into the downstairs. What the hell were we going to say when Tony, Laura and Vickie came home? The five of us had lost all our clothes and money, but they had lost everything including their home.

I looked in the window again and saw a metal lamp melting. It was an inferno inside with solid white hot flames and fleeting sparks of green. The rest was Halloween orange.

We killed two bottles of whiskey, but it didn't make a dent.

By the time the morning birds were singing, there was nothing left except a glowing stone chimney, that skinny two-story monolith, standing over a smoking mound of red hot rubble.

Dawn is fine when you've slept well with a clear conscience, but a dawn like this was a hard thing to face, especially when you're freezing with nowhere to go.

We decided that we'd pile into Don's Volkswagen bug with all the blankets and the sleeping bags, but that didn't work too well. Even with Max comfortably sleeping in the little space behind the back seat, there wasn't enough room to stretch out. That's all we wanted to do. Our bodies were aching.

Loo and I gave up trying to sleep and we left the guys, who had snoozed off. It's a fact that guilt rarely affects a man's sleep.

We decided that we ought to milk the goats, so we went to the barn. In there it was gray and cool and still, with the first glints of the sun shooting stripes of light through the chinks of vertical wood. The cobwebs in the corners swayed a little in a slow breeze and pieces of hay from the loft floated down once in a while. Everything looked soft, as if there were no sharp edges. Morning doves in the rafters murmured and rustled their wings, and the goats were casually chewing hay like it was any normal day. Despite this, I saw there was something accusatory in their eyes. Goats have the strangest eyes in the world; the pupils are slits in bright light; in semi-darkness the pupils are diamond shaped, not unlike snake eyes.

We gave them some oats and sat down, back to back, on the little stool next to them. It is not an easy trick to milk an animal; it had taken me days to learn it from Laura.

After we got a squirting rhythm going, Loo asked the question we'd all been thinking about.

"How do you suppose the fire started?"

"Lord, I don't know," I shook my head slowly. "An act of God?"

"I think we stoked the wood stove too high. The flues were wide open. I remember Tony telling us not to open the flues all the way."

"Yeah?... OH NO!!... Yeah! He did say that, didn't he?" My heart sank. It was our fault. He had told us quickly before he left that with the flues wide open sometimes chunks of burning wood fly up the chimney, because that stove was really too big for that size chimney. It created up drafts of something. Because of this, chunks of burning wood could fall on the roof.

"But who opened the flues all the way?"

"Nobody's going to admit to that," Loo said, "and there's no point accusing anybody now."

She was right, of course.

After we milked the goats, we dropped into the hay and fell asleep from sheer exhaustion.

I guess it was around noon when I heard Tony and Laura's pickup come rumbling down the gravel drive. Loo and I hopped up from the hay and stopped the truck before it could go any further. From the distance of the barn to the house, one could only see the top of the chimney over the edge of huge Douglas firs.

The truck radio was blaring some country hit, but they turned it off when they took a look at our faces. They knew there was something wrong.

How in the world does one tell a friend that their house burned to the ground?

Loo started. "The house... it caught on fire... and..."

Tony and Laura just stared at both of us.

"It burned to the ground," I said, and looked down at my sooty cowboy boots.

"No it didn't," laughed Laura. Loo and I looked at each other. Hey, maybe it didn't, I thought. Maybe it was just a dream. Maybe over the hill the house was standing like it always had. I looked at the chimney top. Maybe the whole house was under it, with Don cooking soup at the stove and Howard sitting in the livingroom reading. Maybe it hadn't burned down, just like Laura said.

Loo and I got in the truck and we slowly drove up the drive. The whole scene opened up after the trees and it looked so bad. Laura began to cry, and Tony just stopped driving and turned off the motor.

Two hours later, Vickie came home and she was hysterical when she saw it. By then Tony was walking around in the rubble with the bottoms of his boots smoking, looking for stuff from upstairs.

We slept in the barn that night. Tony put up a huge tent and piled hay bundles around it for insulation from the cold. We cooked our dinner outside over a fire. Fortunately we had saved all those sleeping bags, so it was really cozy, all of us in a row sleeping in the tent. We even laughed a lot that night.

The next day we started work on the log cabin. I had the job of chinking the logs with a combination of horse shit and mud. With all of us working furiously we could have the place built in a matter of days.

Word got out in the town that our house had burnt down; and later that very day, families came from all over with food, and warm clothes, and more tools. They just picked up hammers and chainsaws, and then there were twenty people working. We finished that house in three days.

Then we started in on the tree house. That was a bigger task, but after another two weeks or so, both the houses were really in order, and that's when I decided to move on. I hated to leave, but I had the feeling that

Tony and Laura and Vickie wanted to get on with their lives without a bunch of guests. Don and Loo had already gone two days before, and Howard was only going to stay another day or two, and then return to Provincetown. I didn't want to go back to Provincetown immediately, but I didn't have any money, and there really wasn't anybody to ask for some to borrow.

Howard was the only one, really. He'd saved his bag from the fire. It had been downstairs. He loaned me fifty dollars and that seemed like plenty. Don had given me some cocaine to sell when I got where I was going. Laura had offered me some from her bank account but I just couldn't take it.

The night before I left, Tony went into the mountains and shot a bear, and we invited everybody from the town who'd helped us for a grand outdoor bear feast.

Before we skinned him, we gave him his last rites. He was so big and handsome with gigantic brown eyes. We all started crying before our guests came.

I left the next day with Max on my back. Somebody from town was going to Eureka, California, a two day drive, so I drove with him that far, and hitchhiked the rest of the way to San Francisco to visit Divine.

But that's a whole other story.

The Stone Age — Sicily — 1976

There are plenty of sex perverts in Sicily; all of them are men. The whole island, as I see it, is a man's primordial porno playground. The place pulsates with the vibes of undulating male loins.

Of course it's all very hush-hush… all very covert and Catholic. I don't think Sicilian wives are very much aware of this, but who really knows the truth except the priests in the confessional booths?

Wherever we went, we were plagued with randy dandies and horny honchos. Guys were always walking along beside us whispering in dialect about their balls and other organs. Along paths in mountains, where we thought we might find respite from all these biological urges, we would see lust areas in the underbrush where sex parties took place at night. We'd always catch a few guys jerking off in the magenta crush of bougainvillea blossoms.

They followed us everywhere; the fact that we were both blonds had something to do with it. The fact that were lesbians on a honeymoon didn't make much difference to them. Four year old Max was with us too, and that didn't deter them either. Maybe they thought he was a very short pubescent girl. Everyone is short in Sicily anyway.

"I'm tired of walking everywhere in this country," Shaggy said.

"I want to go back to the beach," Max whined.

"I just thought you two might want to walk in the mountains for a change," I said. We were walking up a quiet road into the hills. A boy, barely nine years old, pulled up to us on his Piaggio. His motor was hot. He smiled and said something to us.

"Another pervert," Shaggy said. She knew a little bit of the Sicilian dialect from her mother.

"Whadhesay?" Max asked.

"He was telling us about his personal history," I told Max. "Just ignore him."

We decided to rent a car to get around. After being haunted by guys on Vespas and wild groups of cruisers in Fiats everyday, we thought it would be a better idea. We went to a fly-by-night rental place where there were rows of navy blue Fiats waiting in the sun. To rent us the car the man didn't want money or a credit card; we didn't own one anyway and he didn't know what a credit card was.

"One of you will have to leave a passport," he said in his English. Since Shaggy and I had both given our passports to the pension people, Max's passport was the only one would could give him. That was fine with him. "Mario, the man who runs this place, isn't here now, but he'll take care of the money when you bring the car back. Okay?" he said. That sounded fine.

I jumped into the driver's seat and we barreled off. I loved the car. It was the size of an ordinary kitchen table. It handled like a small bathtub with wheels. Now the horny grape growers and olive farmers wouldn't bug us. We would leave them in the dust. We were mobile.

We still ran into problems when we stopped at intersections. There'd always be a man on a corner who would notice us quickly and he would immediately expose himself by dropping his scrubbed drawers around his ankles. In Sicily, all the men's underpants are very clean. Their wives or mothers don't have much else to do during the day except wash clothes.

"I'm beginning to think there's sexual repression in Sicily," I said as I turned the corner away from the butt-naked man.

"They seem healthy to me," Shaggy said, looking back at him while he was pulling up his pants.

"Maybe it's us," I said. "Maybe our clothes are too tight or something."

"I think it's because we're Americans and we're blond," Shaggy said.

"Maybe it's your eye makeup," Max said from the back seat. He was pretty astute for a four year old.

We were staying in a pension in a little town called Rocalamare. It consisted of that pension, an empty beach, a restaurant, a cigarette store, a grocery store, and a variety store. The population was about eighty children, forty-five men and three fat women. We spent most of our days on the sun-baked beach next to the placid water of the Ionian Sea, burning the retinas of our eyeballs reading books to fill the vacant hours. Rocalamare was very close to Taormina, where we had wanted to stay because of the annual Taormina Film Festival. We had plans to meet with some German independent filmmakers there but because of the festival there weren't any vacancies in any of the pensions we could find in Taormina.

The first night of the festival, we drove into Taormina. The festival films were all shown in an ancient Greek amphitheater which sat on the edge of a mountain overlooking the sea and the active volcano Mount Etna. We found our German director friends there.

"Ve von't hf time fa dinna," Werner said as he ran along with his Japanese wrist watch. "But I haf dis bottle orf red vine. Ve'll haf dis, no? Ve'll vatch the films, den maybe ve eat somesing afta, no?"

None of the films made any sense to us. We'd

forgotten that they were all in Italian. Even the German and American films were dubbed in Italian. I hated dubbed films, even when they're dubbed in my own language; it just ruins everything.

By the time the films were over, all the restaurants everywhere were closed and the opening night festival party was a flop, so Shaggy and I returned to the Rocalamare pension, drunk and hungry.

I'd left Max there with a ten year old daughter of the pension owner and there he was sitting in the big family kitchen under a faulty florescent light at a high marble table with skinny white cats scattered around eating cold pasta on newspapers. Max was drawing on butcher paper with waxy crayons.

The ten year old babysitter looked like she was about forty years old. It occurred to me maybe she wasn't a child at all, just a short adult. She had been waiting on tables in the family restaurant for five years, all the kids waited on tables in Sicily. Waitress jobs make girls look old before their time.

"I don't like it here," Max said the next day, sitting on the bed crying.

"I don't either," said Shaggy. We started to pack. I didn't really like it either.

We paid our bill and said goodbye to the family, then we packed up the Fiat and left to return the car to the rental place. On the way, we came to some railroad tracks where the red lights were flashing and the bells were bonging. A train was coming. I stopped the car and waited for it to pass.

I had stopped the car in the wrong place. The red striped two ton metal pole that lowers automatically to warn cars on road crossings was slowly smashing the roof of our Fiat. We were wedged under it.

I felt like a complete asshole while the people in other cars laughed at us. I tried to back up, but we were pinned. As the pole squeeched metal on metal, I looked at Max in the back seat to see if he was okay. He was laughing. Shaggy was laughing. The roof was smashing in.

"Get out of the the car," I screamed. "We're going to get crushed." They weren't taking this very seriously, but they jumped out. The car was shaking and its steel body was whining under the weight. Then the pole stopped descending. We waited. After the train passed, the pole lifted and the little blue Fiat bounced up into position on its rubber tires. The roof was all smashed in, sway-backed, like a birthday cake someone had fallen into.

"We're going to jail now," I said. "We don't have the money to pay for these damages."

"Get back in the car," Shaggy said. "We'll take our chances at the rental joint."

"Don't mention the roof until they do," I told both of them.

"Maybe we could just leave the car there with some money and keys in an envelope," Shaggy said.

"Let's just leave it by the side of the road," Max said.

"You're forgetting about your passport," I told him.

We drove the car back to the rental lot. I turned off the ignition and sat there for a few minutes. I knew we would all go to jail or something and this was our last day of freedom.

I walked into the office and met Mario, who was sitting behind the desk. I handed him the keys.

"Okay, let's take a look to see how many kilometers are on the car," he said and slid off his seat. He stood no taller than my waist! I couldn't believe it! Mario was a midget! This was divine providence! He looked the car over, checked the kilometers, kicked the tires... but he couldn't see the top of the car. He was too short.

He gave us back Max's passport and we paid the small sum for the rental and left.

There's an old superstition in Sicily about seeing a midget. It brings luck.

Go-Going—New York & New Jersey—1978-79

In the beginning I just couldn't bring myself to do floor
work. Bumping and grinding while laying on the floor
looked completely ludicrous to me.

I would have made more tips if I had; the girls who
did floor work always had stacks of one dollar bills in
their G-strings. They wore the money like a tiny green
fringe tu-tu flapping around their hips.

Those girls brought their own personal floor mats on
stage with them for their half-hour sets. They'd just
unroll their fake fur bathroom rugs on the stage floor
and lay down and start undulating.

It seemed so inane... convulsing there on a dirty
dynel shag pad on a "stage," which was usually nothing
but a flimsy fly-by-night platform the size of a dinner
table, while stone-faced male loners sat in a circle
around it, clutching their overpriced drinks, watching
intently this twitching female flesh parcel.

No, that wasn't for me. I just danced. On two feet.

I had decided to topless go-go dance when I first
moved to New York from Provincetown. It wasn't

something I especially wanted on my resume but I had been casting around, looking for work… something to pay the bills while I was making a start at designing clothes, searching film parts and writing. I was down to thirty-seven dollars. That kind of money doesn't go far in New York, especially when you have a kid.

I'd tried waitressing when I was sixteen and found out fast it wasn't my calling in life. I always screwed up. People were always bitching about the missing side orders. I spilled everything, had a lot of walk-outs. It's a horrible job, demanding, demeaning. I started hating people. I wound up throwing food.

I'd worked in offices when I was eighteen, and that always turned into a fiasco; anyway the pay was so low and it took all day, five days a week. I needed some kind of job that didn't have such long hours and paid really well.

A go-go friend suggested dancing. She gave me her agent's name. I got the job.

The agent was straight out of a cheesy '50s gangster B movie, second generation Italian, the good-looking-twenty-years-ago type, flare collared polyester Nik-Nik shirt, pasta belly, lots of big rings on the pinkies.

He sat in a greasy office filled with cigar smoke, pictures of broads on the walls, the telephone ringing.

Every Monday the place was packed with girls getting the next week's bookings and picking up their checks. He called everybody sweetheart or honey. He was close: all the girls had phoney names like Jujubee, ChiChi, CoCo, Sugarplum, Dumpling, BonBon, Sweetie Pie.

Most topless bars in the city had eight hour work shifts, noon to eight or eight to four a.m. The bars in New Jersey had five hour shifts.

I liked working in Jersey more, where topless was against the law; the dancers had to wear a little something on top. That eliminated my stretch marks and sag problem that came with the pregnancy and breast feeding package. It was less sleazy in Jersey; the bars were local hangouts for regulars; the customers didn't feel like they were getting ripped off because drinks were cheap. Dancers made more money in Jersey anyway, and there, no one would ever recognize me from John Waters movies, not that they did in Manhattan go-go bars, but I always had this horror. People in Jersey didn't go to those kind of movies.

Actually it wasn't a horrible job, when I thought about it. I was just there exercising and getting paid for it. I was never in better shape: tight buns, strong legs, flat stomach. Working in Jersey, I began to wonder why every woman didn't want to go-go.

But then, every time I worked in a bar in Manhattan, I discovered why all over again.

Manhattan go-go bars are really sleazy. The owners sometimes want you to go in the back rooms to do hand

"YOU'RE BEELZEBUB," she screamed at John as we tore down the street.

"Did she read the script or something?" John asked. He was upset.

"She sure did," I said, looking back at her. She was still on the front lawn screaming.

"I guess she didn't exactly love it," he said and laughed.

"Not exactly."

"You shouldn't go back there. You can stay with me," John said.

"Yeah. I can't go back there. Did you hear her? She called you Beelzebub."

"Who's Beelzebub anyway?" John asked.

"One of the devil's footmen," I said.

"Was she serious?"

"She was brought up in the deep south as a Southern Baptist. That was high drama. She's an actress," I told him.

"Maybe I ought to give her a part in the film," he laughed.

"I feel kinda bad just packing up and leaving so fast. You sure it's okay that I stay with you for awhile? I know you're under a lot of pressure with the film right now but Max doesn't cry much. I can put him in a dresser drawer. Dr. Spock says to put your infant in a drawer when you're travelling.

John started laughing, "You're joking."

"ART?!?!?! ART!?!?! THIS ISN'T ART!!" she sputtered, and threw the script at me.

"Mom, hold on. Sit down," I said, but there was no calming her. She has quite a temper, that woman.

"AND YOU'RE GOING TO EXPOSE YOUR POOR DEAR LITTLE BABY TO ALL THIS NONSENSE?!?!? THIS GARBAGE?!??!" THIS IS THE SCRIBBLING OF THE DEVIL HIMSELF... THIS SCRIPT, THIS ART SCRIPT! HA! HA! ART!!!" She was really wild now.

All I could do was start packing. Fast.

I threw Max's clothes in his little bag, grabbed his Pampers box, stuffed my clothes into my suitcase and put Max in my arms.

"WHERE DO YOU THINK YOU'RE GOING?!?!? PUT THAT CHILD DOWN!"

Outside, in the driveway, John innocently started beeping his car horn. I cringed.

"IS THAT MANIAC OUT THERE?!? I'M GOING TO GIVE HIM A PIECE OF MY MIND," she yelled and flew out the front door, me following. I hopped in the car with Max and my bags before she reached it.

"Make tracks, John," I said to him. "My mother's on the warpath."

He sped down the driveway. My mother was standing on the front lawn flailing her arms around.

"You're not supposed to close the drawer or anything," I said.

He just kept laughing.

We went to the farm from there and got ready to shoot the chicken scene in the chicken coop. It went well, but we had to reshoot four times, the chickens weren't too compliant. Danny (Crackers) had to kill eight or nine of them; I didn't watch him slice off the heads.

Just as David had said, even without heads they were a lively nasty bunch of fowl, flopping and kicking with all their might. I got completely scratched up by their sharp claws. I was getting hurt for real. I'd underestimated these chickens, even while I was feeling sorry for them.

In the next scene Max was great as Little Noodles. He upstaged even the bulldykes.

Later on, after we finished for the day, with the sun sinking beyond the horizon of winter's leafless trees, we roasted all those chickens, had a big feast for the whole cast and crew. Those chickens I'd felt so sorry for earlier sure were delicious.

British Columbia — 1972

I accidentally burned a friend's house to the ground once. The friend didn't approve. True, it wasn't entirely my fault; I was a guest along with three other guests.

The friend was away for the burning that evening, Friday the thirteenth, November 1972.

I had just left Baltimore after filming *Female Trouble* with John Waters and needed a vacation somewhere other than were I was living, Provincetown, Massachusetts.

I went to visit my friends, Tony and Laura, in British Columbia, right on the edge of the Canadian Rockies, minutes from the Kootney River, outside a little town called Nelson.

They were married and it was their first home. They lived there with a girl named Vickie who was part owner. There were three bedrooms upstairs, with quite a view from the guest bedroom, where Max, Howard, Don, Loo and I slept in two beds.

It was land with no boundaries, no discernable perimeters anyway, and there was a barn where the jobs on the creeps. They made customers buy outrageously priced little bottles of champagne; some managers demanded that you "flash"... show your puss, when they knew you could get busted for that.

Of course, right over on the next block a guy could walk into a strip joint and get a bird's eye view deep into the internal structure of a vagina for a dollar; in fact, he could stick his nose right in if he wanted, but in topless places, because they served liquor, nothing like this was supposed to go on.

I was working the day shift at the Pretty Purple Pussy Cat, doing my half-an-hour-on, half-an-hour-off. I was working the same half-hour as Taffy, on stages facing each other. The other two girls, Marshmallow and Lollipop, went on after us. With those names, the place could have been a candy store.

Taffy was wallowing on her bathroom rug, with all the customers at her stage, ogling. She had piles of bills tucked in everywhere, mostly ones, but when somebody wanted her to flash, she'd do it for a five.

I was on the other stage, knocking myself out doing flips, splits, high kicks, triple spot turns, with nobody watching me, thinking that somebody with respect for a real dancer would soon toss me some fifty dollar bills. Nobody did.

I watched Taffy. She was laying there pumping her hips and looking right into the eyes of the men. She was turning them on, obviously.

I was exhausted. I'd been up since seven-thirty getting Max to school; then I had this early interview at Macy's to show some buyer a couple of silk blouses I'd designed. After that, I'd gone for a cold reading for some low budget independent cable TV movie.

All I wanted to do was lie down.

When the half-hour was over, I put my little mini-dress over the pink sequined G-string and got off the stage. In Manhattan the dancers are required to hustle drinks from the customers... or at least try. Nobody was buying drinks for me, but Taffy called me over to sit next to her and a customer.

"Buy her a drink," Taffy told the guy and he ordered me vodka soda.

Taffy pulled her chair next to mine.

"Sweetheart, I've been watching you bust your ass over there and you ought to give it a rest, girl. You ain't making no tips. Look here," she looked down at her G-string, "I got a mess of money here," she flipped through the bills hanging on her hips, "and I got more in my pockets here." She put her hands in her mini-dress pockets and pulled out handfuls of ones and fives, even a lot of tens and twenties. "And I didn't make this working too hard."

"For some reason," I told her, "I just can't bring myself to lie down up there. It looks so stupid... I mean, you don't look stupid, the idea is so stupid."

"I know just what you mean," she said. "I used to feel the same way when I started working these bars, but you get over it."

She lit a cigarette and put her Revlon Cherries in the Snow lips to my ear.

"Look," she whispered, "these guys just want to look at something they can fantasize about. They like to feel horny, it makes them happy."

"I think I'd feel like an asshole," I said.

"Oh shit, forget it. You want to make money or not? Just try it next set. Lay there and look right into their eyes. Remember to do that part, otherwise it doesn't work. You have to make it personal."

The next set I took my scarf on stage with me and I laid it on the floor. Nobody would want to lay on the slimy platform without something under them.

Feeling dumb, I got on the scarf and put my head back and looked at the ceiling while I did some sort of cold Jane Fonda-type floor workouts. There was a customer sitting there in front of me but he didn't look very interested.

"That ain't it," Taffy yelled to me from across the room. She pointed at her eyes.

So I made myself look into this guy's eyes. It worked immediately. He started peeling off the ones and handing them to me. This made me start putting some sex into the workout. I undulated all over the place, just like an eel in heat.

Other customers started moving over to my stage looking for something hot, I guess. They loved it hot.

By the end of the set I had twenty or thirty dollars and it was so easy on the heel bunions and the toe corns, so relaxing for the calf muscles. Wow! What a job!

"I should'nta told you nothin'," Taffy said, "you took all my paying customers."

So I had graduated. Every working day I'd dance the first half of the set and when I got tired I'd just lie down and stare into eyes and pump the hips, do leg lifts, things like that.

I worked this job for a year or so, two or three days a week, saved some money. I worked in Jersey mostly, taking the Path train to Newark, and then taking a cab. There weren't too many problems except for having too much to drink during the day. It would be an ideal job for an alcoholic, I often thought.

One day I was working in a Manhattan bar where sometimes the owner would try to act like a pimp. I hated working there, but it was the only place the agent had left on a Wednesday, since I forgot to see him on Monday booking day.

I was doing floor work in front of a customer and he was handing me dollars. He asked me to sit and drink with him when I came off the stage. So I did.

He was a young guy from Brooklyn, a blond meathead who wasn't unlike all the other meatheads who hung around go-go bars everyday. He was buying vodkas, and he was getting drunk and I was getting drunk. He was telling me his life, his astrological sign, the standard rap.

"Ya read about dem tree peoples killed in Brooklyn yestaday?" he asked. "Was inna Post and da News. Sawr it onna tube too, late night news."

"Yeah, I saw it. Terrible," I said. I had seen it. Pretty grisly, it was too. Torsos in green garbage bags, with treasure hunt notes leading to the heads, which were in black garbage bags.

"I did dat," he smiled. "I killed dem. Cut 'em up. Waddn't too easy eitha."

I turned and looked at him very closely. He was proudly smiling but he looked really serious, although he didn't look like a killer, except maybe for his eyes... but then I don't know if I'd ever looked in the eyes of a killer before.

"You didn't do that," I laughed.

"Oh yeah, I did. It kinda bodda me a lill, but dey was assholes. Ya don know. When dey died der was no human lives lost. Dey was animals. Deserved it. Fugging animals." He looked into his sixth vodka and drained it.

When he started to cry, I half believed his story.

What could I say? Could I say something like: "Oh, don't feel so bad. Tomorrow's another day. Forget all

about these heads and bodies. You're just depressed."
That wasn't really appropriate under the circumstances.

"Ya know, I have dis gun, heer, in ma coat," he
looked around to see if anybody was watching, then
withdrew it quickly and showed it to me.

I was beginning to believe him.

"I have dis index finga too from onna dem animal."
He pulled out a plastic ziplock bag with a human finger
in it. The blood was caked around the stump. He put it
away fast.

I think I just sat there staring at his pocket for a
while.

"Well ......" I just didn't know what to say. What
could I say? What would be the right thing to say when
something like this happens?

Maybe I could say, "Oh. Isn't that interesting
looking!"

I thought that maybe I should say something to the
bouncer though, but this guy would figure it out if I told
him I was going to the bathroom and instead started
whispering to the tough guy in the corner. He might go
on some wild shooting spree. No, I couldn't say
anything. I just drank the rest of my vodka and tried not
to stare at him aghast.

The other dancer, Pepper, got off the stage and it was
my turn.

"I need to talk ta ya sommoor," he said. "Comon back
afta. I'll be real pissed if ya don't."

I certainly didn't want to piss him off.

"Don't worry, I'll be right here in front of you and I'll sit with you again after my set," I said and he smiled.

If I hadn't been slightly drunk I think I might not have been able to dance, maybe not even able to undulate on the floor. Considering the circumstances, I was very nonchalant, but I decided not to do any floor work in front of him now. I didn't want to get this guy aroused or anything. I just stepped around on the stage while he smiled at me.

Pepper started to sit down with him to ask him for the drink.

"Gedda fug outta heer," he pushed her away. Then he felt bad. "Hey look, girlie, I'm sorry, ba I'm savin' my dough fa dis chick heer," he pointed to me. "I like er."

Great. Just great, I thought.

While I was dancing and trying to smile at him, thinking about garbage bags and heads, a bunch of men came in the bar talking to each other.

One of the guys stopped to look at me and he handed me a fifty dollar bill.

"Come have a drink with me after your set," he said and winked. Then he walked to the end of the bar and sat down with his buddies. They were all talking to the owner and looking at the girls, nodding and laughing.

The gesture wasn't unusual, but the fifty was.

I loved the fifty but the killer didn't.

"Ya ain't gonna sit wit im. Are ya?"

"No. Never."

"Yall havta give im bak dat fifty," he looked over at the guys.

"Yeah," I said, "I was going to do that anyway."

Then the bar owner, one of those Grade D bad eggs, walked over to me and whispered in my ear, "This group of guys back there are friends of mine. They want to party with you, Venus and Fever. In the back room. Go there after the set. They got lots of money. We can both make a little."

He walked off before I could tell him I wasn't interested. First of all I didn't go to backrooms and then of course there was this angry young man sitting here...

He was getting angrier by the minute. He'd heard what the owner asked me to do so he kept looking at the guy who gave me the fifty. He clenched his fists, ground his teeth, bit his lip. His face was getting all red. There was going to be trouble.

What could I do? Getting shot or beheaded wasn't the way I had planned to go out. I didn't have many options: (1) I could sit the rest of the evening with the killer, but at closing time he'd probably follow me home. (2) I could maybe call the police, but the killer might see me at the phone, get paranoid, and shoot me. (3) I could go to the bathroom and climb out the window, if only the bathroom had a window. (4) I could quit the job and walk out while the killer was in the bathroom, but he looked like he had a good bladder.

"Hey, ya name again?" the Brooklyn Butcher yelled up at me over the music. I told him.

"Dat ain't ya reel name," he sneered. "Tell me ya reel name."

"That is my real name."

"It ain't," he barked.

"Okay," I said, "you're right. My real name is Charlene Moore." Any name would do. The kid swallowed his next vodka and started on another one, then another. His eyes were very green and the whites were very red after those twelve vodkas.

"I'm gonna tell dat fugging asshole bak dere dat ya sittin wit me afta ya dance." He got up and stumbled to the back of the room. I froze.

When he got there he started poking his finger at this fifty dollar guy. The guy stood there taking all this abuse and then he just hit the kid killer in the face, really hard. The kid butcher fell on the floor, and his gun fell out of his pocket and slid across the carpet, and disappeared under a huge stationary space heater radiator thing.

He saw it when it slid, and they saw it, and everybody pounced on the space heater and started wailing in pain because the heater was so hot.

Then the kid just scrambled for the door and left the bar, fast.

The bouncer and the owner let him run. They all started bending around the heater, but they couldn't find the gun because, first of all, the bar was so dark, and the heater was so wide and hot.

Finally somebody got a broom and pushed it out.

I got off the stage and walked up to them while they were all huddled around the gun. I told them all about the kid, the whole story. Nobody believed me.

The owner took the gun and disappeared into his office; the rest of the guys just started drinking again; the girls started dancing again, so I went back to the stage.

All the party boys forgot about their party even before I finished my set. They left, all fired up, talking about how "they were going to find that little motherfucker."

I made a phone call to the police. I described the kid, told them everything he told me about himself. They weren't too interested until I told them about the finger. I didn't mention the bar or the gun, I just said I met this kid in some restaurant. I told them my name was Charlene Moore. They thanked me and hung up.

That was the last day I worked as a go-go dancer; I never wanted to see any of those sleazy joints again. I didn't want to writhe on another floor in my life. I didn't want to be forced to talk to any more creepy dummies in dark smelly dives; I was perfectly capable of finding creepy dummies on my own time. I didn't want to be in the same room with murderers or birdbrains or desperate people anymore.

After all, I'd made my first fifty dollar bill that day. Not a bad way to finish up.

When I got home I hung up my pink sequined G-string, and there it hangs to this day, gathering dust. It still sparkles just a little when the sun hits it.

Sam's Party—Lower East Side, NYC—1979

It was his party and he'd die if he wanted to.

Sam was that kind of guy. He never let anyone down, especially himself.

This particular party was for his birthday, at the apartment he shared with his lovers, Alice and Tom. All his loyal friends were there, the famous, the infamous, the washouts, the successful rogues, and the types who only have fame after they die. They were the representatives of the New York alternative subculture, the people who went to sleep at dawn. And never held a nine-to-five job because they were too odd looking, or sassy, or over-qualified.

Because Sam had an MFA degree, he never had any money, but he always gave great parties... never pretentious ones, always wild ones. He wasn't short-handed with the food or liquor.

It wasn't even midnight but the party was already jammed and jumping. Alice hadn't even gotten around to lighting the candles on her attempted Cordon Bleu birthday cake when I noticed Sam thanking a rock star for a very small birthday present, one of the many very small presents he'd received all night, yet another glassine bag of heroin, his drug of choice. He'd been using it off and on for the past five years.

He immediately went to the bathroom with Tom and locked the door.

At first no one missed the host. The party was too good. The stereo was blasting rare old hits and obscure unreleased new stuff, people were dancing, laughing, drinking. The layered smoke in the rooms was a gray veil. The place was wall-to-wall celebrities and future stars, who all knew each other and were still speaking.

I was dancing on the sofa when Mary approached me looking a little worried.

"Where's Sam?" she asked. "Have you seen him? I want to light the cake."

"I think I saw him going out for more beer," I lied because Alice didn't like Sam using heroin, especially if she didn't get some of it.

Alice went to the door. Shoeless in her fishnet stockings, she walked out into the misty November night where the party was spilling over into the street.

"Sam?" she screamed lamely into the abyss of the Lower East Side tunnel of tenements. "Sam!?"

"Didn't see him out here, Alice," the people sitting in Sam's blue Pontiac convertible said. There were people on the stairs and on the ledge too, but they hadn't seen him for awhile either. Meanwhile I knew Sam was very busy in the john and by this time there was a line at the locked door. Everyone was getting impatient with their bladders full.

It wasn't three minutes later when Tom slipped out of the bathroom, closing the door behind him and holding the doorknob, making sure no one got in. He looked nervous.

"Hey, Tom, you finished in there or what?" a drag queen film star asked him. She was the first in line.

"Go out on the street and piss," he said just as nicely as he could, and the drag queen thought this was not a bad idea, so she headed for the street. So did a couple of others in line.

While Tom was standing there holding the doorknob, I noticed he looked ashen and awful, like the blood had just drained from his head. Frantically scanning the room, he saw me looking at him and called me over.

"What's wrong, Tom? What's going on?" I asked him after I fought my way through the crowd. Tom's hands, and even his hair-do were trembling. He was sweating all over his party silks.

"Come in here." He wedged the door open so we could squeeze in over protests from the line.

"Hey, come on… man. I was here first, Cookie…"

"Lettus jes take a quick pee."

Inside the bathroom, Sam was lying on the floor in a fetal position. His skin was the color of a faded pair of blue jeans. A syringe and a bunch of crumbled empty glassine bags were on the floor next to him.

"Obviously he's O.D.ing!! Do you know what to do?" Tom was beside himself. He guessed I might know because for years I'd been writing a sort of "health in the face of drug use" column for a downtown newspaper.

"Yeah, don't worry, Tom. There's time before somebody dies shooting too much heroin, it never happens in a flash despite what you've heard. DON'T PANIC! Just go to the kitchen and get some salt... and some ice cubes," I said. "And hurry."

While he was gone, I filled the bathtub with the coldest water possible and tried to lift Sam into it, clothes and all, but he was dead weight, he may as well have been a Buick. I had to wait for Tom but he was probably having a hard time making his way through the mob of plastered party people. When he finally returned, Alice was with him. She started to wail, and tried to kiss Sam awake, which never works.

"Let's get him into the tub," I said, so we lifted him in.

"This water's freezing," Alice cried.

"It's supposed to be," I told Alice.

"I DON'T HAVE TO PEE, I HAVE TO SHIT," someone outside the bathroom door said, banging on the door.

"Do we have any time?" Tom asked.

"He's going to die… on his birthday… he's going to die!" Alice was weeping over the tub, her tears falling on Sam's blue face.

"He won't die," I said.

"WE KNOW YOU'RE DOING DRUGS IN THERE! WE DON'T WANT ANY, JUST LET US PISS!" The banging at the door kept up.

"Any ice cubes?" I asked Tom.

"None. I was fighting over the last ones in somebody's vodka." Tom was sweating again.

"DAMMIT, GUYS… WHAT THE HELL YA DOIN' IN THERE? COUNTING TOILET PAPER SHEETS?" Somebody was really mad.

"What's the ice cubes for?" Alice looked at me with her black eyes, the same kind of orbs on orphans in Keene paintings.

"The cold gets the heart moving. But nevermind, we don't need them really, just hand me the salt and the syringe."

With Sam's teaspoon in my hand, I tried to calmly pour a little salt into it. I couldn't really remember exactly how much to use, but there was little time to belabor the question, so I just used an arbitrary amount and put in some tap water, swished it around, and drew this saline solution into the syringe forgetting about the cotton.

"That works?" Alice demanded.

"That's an antidote?" Tom asked.

"WHAT KIND OF PARTY IS THIS WITH NO BATHROOM FACILITIES!?!" The line was getting riotous.

"You're taking too long, Cookie ..." Tom was wiping the sweat on his forehead with a big beach towel that had a print of a Coca Cola can on it with the words IT'S THE REAL THING.

"He's going to die," Alice was sobbing.

"I told you he's not going to die, Alice!" I said but I was terrified.

"He'll be brain dead!" Alice screamed and threw herself against the toilet.

"He won't be brain dead either," I said, but I wasn't really sure about this part.

I guess I wasn't too convincing about the brain stuff because Alice started again, "He's going to be a vegetable, no better than a cucumber... he's going to ..."

"SHUT UP, ALICE!" I finally screamed while my hands were shaking trying to find a vein that wasn't too scarred up. I put the syringe's dull point into the only clean vein I could find, pulled the plunger back, got blood, and then pushed the salt solution into it slowly.

"Is there any possibility he'll be a vegetable?" Tom asked.

"Look, I don't know! But can you imagine Sam a vegetable? Even if he had half a brain left he'd be smarter than most of the idiots at this party." This vegetable thing was nagging at all of us.

"WE'RE PISSING IN OUR DRAWERS OUT HERE!" the line screamed.

With my thumb on where his pulse should be, I started getting a little scared about the time it was taking for him to come around. It seemed too long, an eternity. I broke out in beads of sweat. Where was his pulse? He didn't even have a faint one.

"Didn't you know how many bags he did?" Alice turned on Tom. "You should have stopped him!"

BANG, BANG, BANG. The people were pounding at the door. "YOU ASSHOLES'VE BEEN IN THERE FOR AN HOUR!"

"I didn't know how many he did. How was I supposed to know?" Tom threw the towel on the tiles.

"You jerk! You could have stopped him!" Alice was hysterical.

"How could anybody stop Sam from doing dope?" he screamed.

"At least he was with him, Alice. What if Sam was in here shooting up all by himself and this happened!" When I said this I felt Sam's pulse returning slightly, then strong, then some pink was coming to his face, edging out the blue, and then there was a sudden movement under his eyelids like his eyeballs were watching some dream go by. In a second his long eyelashes fluttered. He blinked a few times, then opened them.

"Here he comes," I said, relieved. I sank to the toilet seat because my knees were buckling, they'd no longer hold me. Tom and Alice stopped glaring at each other to look at him.

Sam looked around. His eyes focused and he smiled. He became aware of who was in the room with him.

"Oh Sam, honey, baby," Alice was kissing him and crying with joy. She was hugging him, leaning way into the cold water so the bustline of her tight satin dress got all wet.

"WOW! That was pretty good stuff! Can we get some more?"

"YOU HAVE TO BE KIDDING!" Tom wiped the sweat away from his face again with the sleeve of his black sixties silk shirt. He sat down on the floor because his knees had given out too. "You're kidding, right?"

"He's not kidding!" Alice was angry again. "You just O.D.ed, you asshole!" she screamed at Sam.

"You were almost fucking dead, man!" Tom said, laughing nervously.

"I just shot you up with some salt," I said. "Remember it. May come in handy someday."

"How do you feel, Sam? You asshole," Tom smiled at him. "What an asshole," he said to me happily.

"You had us going there for awhile, you jerk," Alice kissed him on his icy lips. "How do you feel?"

121

"I don't think I'm high anymore, dammit." Sam looked mad. Then he looked down at himself while he sat there in the tub. "Hey! You idiots put me in here with my best sharkskin suit on. You could at least have taken it off me!" He stood up in the tub, dripping and wobbling. "I'm freezing. Could you get me some dry clothes, babe?" he asked Alice.

"Of course, sweetheart," she said, and squeezed out the door.

"The two-tone purple one!!" Sam yelled after her.

Someone tried to push in the door when Alice pushed out, but Tom jumped up and stood against it.

"I'M GOING TO PISS RIGHT HERE!" the person said. "I CAN'T HOLD IT ANY LONGER!"

"Go ahead!" Sam shouted back to the guy out there, "make yourself at home."

Obviously he wasn't a vegetable. Sam was Sam again, for better or worse. He took off his suit and wrapped himself in the IT'S THE REAL THING towel. Yeah… it sure is, I thought.

His teeth were chattering while he took off the suit and threw it in the corner. He looked kind of pitiful and still wobbly. It seemed like he had shrunk a little. His fingertips were all wrinkled from the water.

"I feel like shit. I'm not even high anymore!" he grumbled.

I left the bathroom. Some people are never happy.

Outside in the livingroom, the party was still jumping. No one had even suspected that the host had practically died a few minutes ago.

In less than five minutes, I saw Sam with a Nebuchadnezzar of champagne, walking around the dancers filling people's empty glasses. Someone gave him another birthday present, the book by Celine, *Death on the Installment Plan*. Another person handed him a familiar little package, probably more heroin. I shook my head and fought my way to the kitchen. A filmmaker handed me a glass of champagne. I drained it. I remembered that I hated champagne.

"So what have you been doing lately?" this filmmaker asked me.

"Not much," I shrugged. "You know... same old shit..."

The Berlin Film Festival — 1981

The whole time we were flying across the Atlantic I hadn't been nervous at all about my personal stash of drugs that I was carrying inside my overly padded bra.

I got nervous when we walked into the airport in West Germany and I saw all those security men in uniforms with their machine guns.

I had decided to go to the Berlin Film Festival with Beth Channing, the artist and Amos Poe, the filmmaker, who had been invited to show his film *Subway Riders* there.

I had a part in this film. It wasn't a bad part, and I wasn't too horrible in it; the film itself was okay too, although not by any American standards. American audiences always wanted fast tight plots and big budgets and this film didn't have either, but it was viable enough and young Europeans looking for new art would probably think it was inscrutably hip.

Most people in the film world will tell you that the Berlin Film Festival is really fun, more fun than the Cannes Festival, less snooty than the Deauville Festival and less businessy than the LA Festival.

That sounded pretty good to me. Besides, German films were probably better than any other in the world at the time. Fassbinder was tossing his genius around. Herzog was busy influencing all filmmakers in the rest of the world and Schroeder was doing both, but to a more select audience. I wanted to see the stuff hot off the Steenbeck editing machine, fresh in the can, the films that might never get to America and maybe I could get some film work. Maybe. If I hustled. But I wasn't counting too much on that possibility. I suspected that I wouldn't have a lot of time to think about work... too many festival parties... things like that.

Basically I just needed some live European exposure.

All I had to do was get through customs.

This turned out to be harder than anyone would have guessed.

Everything might have gone smoothly if Amos hadn't absentmindedly left his leather quasi-Nazi motorcycle hat on the seat of the plane.

Beth and I waited while he ran back out on the airstrip to get it. Of course it wasn't his fault really, but that put us at quite a disadvantage, since the customs people had nothing to do by the time we reached them. They'd checked all the other passengers.

The beer belly bunch at customs were eager for us. They thought they might have some fun because we didn't look like any of the other passengers.

We expected a little delay, nothing much else. Amos and I didn't know that Beth was carrying marijuana in one of those little gray Tri-X film cannisters.

Unfortunately for her, customs people have been hip to the Tri-X cannister scam since the great marijuana days of the late sixties. They went right for it, found it, and then the place was alive. Suddenly a flurry of dogs and cops were circling in. Dobermans in S&M gear and aging uniformed Hitler youth cracking their knuckles like butchers snapping baby chicken wings gathered around us while visions of gas chambers danced in our heads.

I proceeded to melt into the formica flooring. A puddle of sweat formed around my feet; after all, I was carrying hashish, cocaine, MDA and opium, of course in small amounts, just tads really, but the variety was sure to turn heads once seized.

I wanted to confess, throw in the towel, but the whimpers stuck in my throat. My vocal chords froze in terror and I could only smile like Louis XVI on the guillotine gangplank. With the marble grin of an idiot, I stood there, goose pimples of horror rising on my flesh as the buxom bulldyke cop in full torture drag appeared in white gloves to strip-search me.

In the private room, I began to disrobe. Employing cold weather habits of fashionable bag ladies, and to cut down on the bulk of my suitcase, I was wearing most of the clothes I brought: tights, leg warmers, over-the-knee boots, a dress, two sweaters, a vest, a leather jacket, various fur pieces and a long black coat. It was hell for her. She had to painstakingly inspect every item. She fingered every hemline, felt every bulge, probed the hairs on the endangered species fur. She even dismantled my spike heels.

One can imagine the state I was in. A more stressful situation was difficult to conjure. The sweat was ridiculous.

Remember now that the stash was in my bra. It was no sloppy job. Back in New York I had carefully sliced open one of the seams above the gargantuan tit pads. Between the boob-contoured double foams I had deftly placed in a plastic ziplock bag—all the personal needs of an underground film star.

Right before I removed my bra I realized that this big woman was watching me very intently. I was but a slip of a thing at the time, certainly unwieldy and so top-heavy with those huge fake knockers.

I took off the bra and my pitiful boobs hopped out. They must have looked pretty sad compared to the bra and all its womanly glory.

She looked at my chest, and she looked at the bra, and I noticed a hint of female compassion there. She felt sorry for me, sorry that I should have exposed my secret to her. My secret of little tits.

In deference to me, in pure sympathy, and not to humiliate me any further, she didn't touch the bra. She didn't finger it and probe it the way she had with every other article of my clothing. In her eyes, I saw that she felt sorry for underdeveloped girls. It had not gone unnoticed all her life, probably, that she was too well endowed in that department. She wouldn't embarrass me further by flaunting her superior bustline at me unnecessarily. God's meager dole to me was embarrassing enough.

And I thanked God right there and then. All the padded bras in high school were but a testing ground.

She told me to get dressed and go. She was all through with me.

I stopped sweating then.

Outside the little room, back at customs central, Amos and Beth had both been strip-searched too and Beth was on her way to deportation.

Amos stayed with Beth, waiting until she was safely deported, while I bowed out and proceeded on to Berlin to the hotel to take a bath and wait for Amos there.

I found Johanna Heer, the feisty little Austrian, part businesswoman, part thin-lipped kewpie doll, who was also the camerawoman for Amos' film, at the hotel waiting for us.

"Where's Amos?" Naturally that would be her first question.

I filled her in on the details, and we went to eat, which isn't easy anywhere in Germany because the food is so horrifying. All there is to choose from is pork, pork, pork, prepared in a myriad of different ways.

Later on, during a shopping spree at their German equivalent to Bloomingdales', the Ka Da We department store, I understood all about the German cuisine. There was a whole floor devoted to meat: *Knockwurst, Schinckenwurst, Knockensnicken, Brattenschicken*... endless displays of sausages, pigs in links, hung there bombarding the consciousness, the throwbacks of the Nazi mentality exposed and garnished with green parsley.

Seeing this, I understood the phenomena of Hitler, I knew why Germans HAD to march. Pork makes one want to march.

Anyway, Amos appeared the next day just in time for the opening night party at the huge Intercontinental Hotel, where copious amounts of beer gushed from spouts into endless mugs. What Germany lacks in cuisine is well made up for in the quality of beer. A glass of draft beer is a meal.

I met all the German film stars, people I'd always wanted to have beers with: Udo Kier, Bruno Ganz, Klaus Kinski and the German filmmakers, the ones I'd mentioned before. I was in Aryan heaven.

I became fast friends with Udo Kier, star of Warhol/Morrissey's *Dracula* and *Frankenstein*, star of Fassbinder films, and I fell in love with Tabea Blumenschein, a woman who was Berlin's underground celebrity film queen. I spent a lot of time with Udo and Tabea at Tabea's home when we weren't at a screening of a film during the day or at a festival party at night.

I decided that someday I had to write and direct a film because there are film festivals all year round in all different parts of the world. I could just live from one festival to the next, jetsetting with my can of celluloid, screening the film, looking for distributors, drinking local beverages, partying, living off the fat of moviedom's lush dreamscape, buoyed up into the land of ever-shifting realities where time was measurable only by ninety minute feature-length intervals and space was measurable only by movie houses, star-laden restaurants and festival party halls.

Berlin, like New York, is open all night and the clubs all have that decadent feel of pre-rampage-of-Hitler nights, those kinds of wild nights recreated by Christopher Isherwood in his *Berlin Stories* and the movie *Cabaret*. I wondered if Americas would feel this way about Berlins if they they hadn't seen *Cabaret*.

It's true that all the Festival people except the buyers and sellers were great looking. All native Berlin nightlifers were gorgeous. Even the bookish intelligentsia in this city didn't look boring the way they do in the States, in fact it seemed that everybody I met was the intelligentsia, even the people with the purple mohawks and brown pet rats crawling around in their shirts.

John Waters was at the festival, and we saw a lot of films together, and went to all the night spots doing socio-behavioral studies.

Three days before the end of the festival, I ran into Udo at the festival headquarters.

"You better get out of your hotel room and move the rest of your things into Tabea's, Amos has left the hotel room and gone on to Paris. There's some problem with your bill," Udo said.

"What do you mean... some problems with the bill? The festival pays the hotel bill," I said, but nevertheless I had visions of going to the gas chambers again.

"The festival pays the hotel bill but there's some other things on the bill... I don't know. Go there and talk to the man at the desk," Udo said. "Better hurry. They might confiscate your monkey fur."

I hustled off to the hotel and when I got there the whole staff was in a huff. It turned out that Amos had the false impression that the festival was going to pay for everything, including long distance phone calls and room service. I thought that was fairly reasonable; I would have probably assumed the same, but I hadn't been staying at the hotel at all, just keeping some clothes there and living at Tabea's, so none of the bills were mine.

"You must pay this bill before you leave or we're calling the police," the desk people said, slamming fists on Black Forest wood.

"It's not my bill. I haven't even been here. Talk to the people at the Festival headquarters. I'm not paying this goddamned bill." I ran upstairs to pack. They yelled after me.

"We're calling the police. We're calling the police."

The thoughts of encounters with the German police again made my adrenaline glands go into overdrive. There had to be a way out of this. If I had been wise, I wouldn't have returned to the hotel at all, but I wanted my favorite clothes, the monkey coat, the rest of my money, and of course I needed the return airplane ticket that was lying in the top drawer of the dresser.

I packed in lightning speed, jamming the clothes into the bag and piling on layers that would never fit in the bag. I heaved the whole heavy mass under my arm, the contents spilling out leaving a trail along the hallway to the lobby.

I peeked around the stairwell wall at the front door and the desk. There was absolutely no way of sneaking out the front. In the next second I saw through the big lobby windows, two cop cars pulling up to the entrance, so I ran back upstairs, thinking that there must be a fire exit somewhere.

I found it. Small stairs that led to a basement led to a door that was well bolted. I threw the bolts back, and the door was so heavy, but I got it open finally, only to find a ten-foot tall wire mesh fence, and after that a twelve foot wall with ivy growing on it.

"There's no stopping now," I said to myself as the heavy door closed and locked behind me, so I threw my heavy bag over the wire mesh fence and scaled it, ripping my blue leather skirt up to the hip on the barbs at the top, while the fence wobbled with my weight. I jumped down and then looked at the wall. What the hell was I going to do? I could use the ivy plants to climb the wall only if they were older plants with thick vines.

I quickly did some horticultural investigations and figured the vines were just old enough, so I threw the bag over the side. That took a few tries, and when I finally got it over I didn't hear it hit the ground on the other side for a very long time. That wasn't great. Once I was on top of the wall, where would I be?

I started up the vines and halfway I had to take off my boots and throw them over. It was easier in stocking feet.

On the way up I couldn't help thinking how perfect the scenario was. There I was in Berlin scaling a wall in fear, skirt all ripped, stockings now in tatters. It was the famous nail-biter scene from some anti-communist film: Youngish East Berliner female climbs the Berlin Wall to get into West Berlin with the East Berlin police firing machine guns at her. We all know this.

I got to the top of the wall. Below me on the other side was a construction site, a deep wide pit, the future basement of some housing development or something. Far below in the dirt was my bag and my boots. Now what?

If I walked along the edge of the wall far enough, there was a place to jump down on a pile of concrete blocks. From there I could climb down and get my stuff, but then how would I get out of the pit and onto the street? I'd figure that out then. If I had to, I'd sleep in the pit and the construction workers could let me out in the morning.

I forged ahead, got my stuff and found a way out of the pit, but then there was another wire fence to the street and a few people were walking by. How embarrassing, I thought, a chic underground film star climbing a fence out of a pit in Berlin. How could I live this one down?

When I got to the fence, all dirty and ripped up, I yelled to a passerby who was gawking at me anyway. He could help.

"*Sprechen Si Englisch?*" I yelled frantically, glancing around for patrolling cop cars.

"Yes, but only a little. I studied it when I was..."

"Never mind," I cut him off. "Can you just help me? Take this bag and then catch me when I jump down into the street." I started climbing the fence, skirt flapping in the breeze. Did I have underwear on? I wondered.

He helped me, he wasn't fazed a bit, just curious. Germans are always trying to understand the intellectual significance of every action.

"Now can you hail a taxi for me?" I asked him and looked down at myself in way of explanation. No cabbie would pick me up looking like this. There were no cabs. I expected the cops any second so I hid in the shadows waiting. Still, there were no cabs.

I saw a bus in the distance. I ran out into the street and flagged it down. Anything to get out of this neighborhood. When I crawled on board, the busdriver and the passengers were aghast. Nobody in Germany walked around half-naked from the waist down, barefoot, dirty, in the middle of February.

"Just get me to a taxi stand," I said as I hunted for some correct change.

Interminable minutes droned on. I stood there in the front of the bus, covered in dirt, humiliated, and the bus was alive with whispers. Everybody on the vehicle was talking about me.

Suddenly I saw a cab and I screamed for the bus driver to stop. He was very happy to let me out and I threw myself in front of the cab. The cabbie almost wouldn't let me in but I pleaded and showed him a handful of money.

While driving to Tabea's flat, I was thinking about how I was going to strangle Amos Poe when I got back to the States.

"Cookie, what happened to you?" Tabea asked, laughing, as she let me in the door. She was frying up some sausages while the music of Wagner was blaring on the radio.

"I just climbed the Berlin Wall."

My Bio—Notes on An American Childhood

The year I was born, 1949, the North Atlantic Treaty was signed, the Dutch were ousted from Indonesia and the first Russian nuclear bomb was exploded. So what. It didn't happen in America so who cared? Not me. I was too small.

I cared about the flannel blanket which I sat on naked under a Norway maple tree in my Baltimore backyard. I cared about the kitchen sink that I was small enough to take a bath in, and I cared about my right thumb, which I sucked.

Somehow I got the name Cookie before I could walk. It didn't matter to me, they could call me whatever they wanted.

In 1949 my eyes were the same size as they are now, because human eyes do not grow with the body; they're the same size at birth as they will always be.

That was 1949.

In 1959, with eyes the same size, I got to see some of America travelling in the old green Plymouth with my parents who couldn't stand each other, and my brother and sister who loved everyone. I remember the Erie Canal on a dismal day, the Maine coast line in a storm, Georgia willow trees in the rain, and the Luray Caverns in the Blue Ridge mountains of Virginia where the stalagmites and tites were poorly lit.

Unfortunately I remember all too well Colonial Williamsburg, where the authentic costumes were made out of dacron and poly and the shoes were Naugahyde. I remember exactly how much I detested seeing these fakers in those clothes, as I was very concerned with detail. Even more than the outer garments, I imagined that, of course, they weren't wearing the historically correct undergarments. I knew in my heart that, for instance, the person who was dressed up to look like the 1790's blacksmith was wearing Fruit of the Loom underpants. Hiding under colonial skirts that the women wore were cheap 79 cent nylon pantyhose from Woolworth's. This bothered me very much.

My father's travel itinerary was mighty strange. We visited a salt peter mine somewhere in the woods of someone's rundown farm. It was listed in some defunct tour guide manual, but it wasn't much of a tourist attraction, maybe because salt peter has such a bad name. Still does. It's the stuff used in American cigarettes to make them burn up faster.

Actually the salt peter cave was really quite beautiful because it was all white salt crystals that would have sparkled if it had been a sunny day. The farmer who showed us the little cave had to keep a dirty red checkered oilcloth over the entrance so the crystals wouldn't dissolve in the rain.

At home in the quasi-country lands of Baltimore county I would spend idle summer months in the woods behind my parent's house. In these woods was a strange railroad track, where a mystery train passed through a tunnel of trees and vines twice a day, once at 1 p.m. and then again in the opposite direction at 3 p.m. I would climb a steep hill which sat right on the tracks and I would look down into the smoke stack and always the black smoke would settle on my white clamdiggers.

For miles and miles in the direction the train was heading there was nothing except a seminary and an insane asylum, so naturally my assumption was that one of the boxcars was full of loons anxious to be committed. The other car was, of course, full of future priests, students of theology, who, as everyone knows, have to use public transportation because they're far too religious to drive their own cars. The 3 p.m. train would return the other way carrying the dirty laundry: I guessed both boxcars were full of stained straight jackets and sweaty clerical collars. There was always a caboose full of shirtless men with fistfuls of cards, probably playing strip poker. They would always wave as they went chugging by.

In these woods I found lots of pets. I brought home box turtles; one I named Fidel, because I had a crush on Castro at the time. My sister named another one Liberace, because she had a crush on him.

Fidel, the turtle, was great in captivity. He used to crawl up into Jip's dog food bowl and chow down. Jip would get angry and run over to the bowl and growl at the turtle who was eating all his food, but Fidel ignored Jip. He kept eating. Turtles are the plodders in nature's scheme. They're the ones that know the term "easy does it," the ones that don't let minor setbacks and petty jealousies bother them much. It's obvious when you study a turtle. Their skin is as thick as linoleum and their shells are as hard as the undergirdings of a concrete overpass. My parents hated Fidel, only because of his name; they named one of the turtles Joe McCarthy, to keep a political balance. There were 11 box turtles roaming around in the house one summer.

I would also bring home black snakes and tadpoles that turned into frogs all over the house. Once I brought home a nest of baby opossums that turned out to be rats. My mother was not amused by this.

One day, along the tracks, I unearthed a yellow jacket hive while I was rearranging boulders. Stung seventeen times, the doctors didn't see much hope for me, but I recovered.

After facing death, I became a young novelist and wrote a book about the Jonestown Pennsylvania flood in 1830 something, where Clara Barton threw her weight around. I did research. Clara Barton was the American version of Florence Nightingale. She was a nurse in Gettysburg during the Civil War, just like Ms. Nightingale in the Crimean War... or some old war over there.

On Barton's hemlines there were always blood stains and she carried morphine in her pockets. She wasn't as much of a tramp as Florence Nightingale, though, Nightingale spread syphilis to all the European soldiers, but Barton was probably an American pioneer celibate.

The book was 321 pages long, and I finished it the day before my 11th birthday. I'd heard somewhere that the girl who wrote *Black Beauty* was 11, so I wanted to be the youngest novelist in the world.

I didn't have any idea how to get the book published, so I typed it all up, stapled it together, cut up some beer case cardboard, covered this with white butcher paper and Saran wrap. Fashioned after any legitimate library book, I smuggled it into the library and put it on the shelves in the correct alphabetical order. I never saw the book again.

I learned early that writing was hard on the body. Blood turns cold and circulation stops at the typewriter; the knee joints solidify into cement, the ass becomes one with the chair, but I kept writing.

One Sunday, around this time, my brother died. It happened at the railroad tracks. He was climbing a dead tree and it fell on him. It was quick. He was fourteen. He hadn't seen a whole lot and he saved himself a myriad of future problems. He was one of those kind of people who was too sensitive to hang around for long.

My mother's hair went gray practically overnight, but she dyed it black again after awhile.

"Whenever you're depressed, just change your hair color," she always told me, years later, when I was a teenager. I was never denied a bottle of hair bleach or dye. In my closet there weren't many clothes, but there were tons of bottles.

Ten years later, at the beginning of 1969, I was in a mental hospital in San Francisco, having been committed by my roommates. They did it out of desperation; they'd tried everything including potatoes, nature's tranquilizers: au gratin, mashed, boiled, baked and fried.

All that you've heard about mental hospitals is true. Patients cut paper dolls, and they weave baskets, and they have a lot of wild fun late at night when there aren't any doctors around. Crazy people have a hard time sleeping at night.

In the wee hours there were only nurse's aids and bouncers. The bouncers were huge, just like bouncers at sleazy bars. When a late night gathering would get too out of control, the bouncers would bodily pick up the loudest of the lot and throw them into solitary confinement. I found out that solitary confinement isn't as romantic as it sounds.

One day I accidentally had shock therapy, when I got in the wrong line. I thought I was waiting for drugs. It's the truth.

You have heard a lot of bad things about shock therapy, perhaps from reading too many renditions of the Frances Farmer story, and you may have an opinion about it. But it really isn't as bad as you may think. It really isn't so horrible, as a matter of fact, it's rather pleasant, because it eradicated from my memory all the contents of stupid literature, the required reading forced on me by liberal English Lit. teachers in school. It all came back in a few months.

In this hospital everyone got lots of thorazine, stellazine, and hot chocolate. The hot chocolate was doled out constantly after the sun went down for the patients who couldn't sleep, and that was everyone. Even after megadoses of tranquilizers, the brain pans were still overflowing; the cogs of wild imaginations were still whirling, so there were lots of loons walking around like the people from the film *The Night Of The Living Dead*. Everyone clutched their styrofoam cups of hot chocolate. The floors were sloshed up from the spills; after all those tranquilizers, people got pretty sloppy.

I met some very entertaining people there.

After two months in the California hospital, I was sent to a Maryland hospital. The staff of doctors wanted me to be near the place I was born and raised.

And wouldn't you know it, ironically, they sent me to the very hospital that was in the woods behind my parent's house. I found out that the mystery train, the one whose smokestack used to sooty up my clamdiggers, didn't stop at the mental hospital at all, but I could see it from my barred windows as it passed at 1 p.m. and then again at 3 p.m. Somehow, seeing this train did bring me down to earth again. I got better.

In the caboose of the train, the same shirtless men were playing the same games, just as they had ten years before.

Ten years later, after moving around in the world and then to New York, I got a phone call from my mother on a rainy Sunday. She told me that my father had just died when the Plymouth ran over him in the driveway. My mother got out the hair dye bottle again.

No, some things never change.

Even if they do, it doesn't matter; you can cover all of it with black hair dye.

COOKIE MUELLER

Last Letter — 1989

Last Letter — 1989

"It's like war time now," my aunt told me a few weeks ago. She lived in France during World War II. "You young people are losing friends and relatives just as if it were bullets taking them away."

She's right, it's a war zone, but it's a different battlefield. It's not bullets that catch these soldiers, and there's no bombs and no gunfire. These people are dying in a whisper.

In 1982, my best friend died of AIDS. Since then there have been so many more friends I've lost. We all have. Through all of this I have come to realize that the most painful tragedy concerning AIDS death has to do with something much larger than the loss of human life itself. There is a deepening horror more grand than the world is yet aware. To see it we have to watch closely who is being stolen from us. Perhaps there is no hope left for the whole of humankind, not because of the nature of the epidemic, but the nature of those it strikes.

Each friend I've lost was an extraordinary person, not just to me, but to hundreds of people who knew their work and their fight. These were the kind of people who lifted the quality of all our lives, their war was against ignorance, the bankruptcy of beauty, and the truancy of culture. They were people who hated and scorned pettiness, intolerance, bigotry, mediocrity, ugliness, and spiritual myopia; the blindness that makes life hollow and insipid was unacceptable. They tried to make us see.

All of these friends were connected to the arts. Time and history have proven that the sensitive souls among us have always been more vulnerable.

My friend Gordon Stevenson, who died in 1982, was a filmmaker. His insights turned heads. With his wife, Muriel, who starred in his low-budget films, he was on the road to a grand film future, one that would serve to inspire and influence a lot of people. When Muriel died in a car accident in Los Angeles, it wasn't long after that Gordon started getting sick.

We thought it was mourning that was wasting him, until he was eventually diagnosed and admitted to the hospital with AIDS. He demanded that I didn't visit him there, and I honored his wish, so we talked on the phone every day and he wrote me one letter.

It was written on his own paper, with his designed letterhead: a big black heart, inscribed with the words Faith, Hope and Charity on a background of orange. It was the last letter I received from him. He died the day I got it. I still have it, it's all frayed but the message is crisp.

Dear Cookie,

Yesterday when I talked to you on the phone, I didn't know what to say... Yes you're right, all of us "high riskers" have been put through an incredible ordeal—this is McCarthyism, a witch hunt, a "punishment" for being free thinkers, freedom fighters, for being "different."

I think if you told kids that measles was caused by excessive masturbation, and were made to wear T shirts to school that said "contaminated" so that no one would sit near them or play with them, and then put in a hospital ward with other measles patients to have swollen glands ripped out, spots cut off, radiation bombardment, and tons of poison to kill the measles, all the while their parents telling them it serves them right, masturbation is a sin, they're gonna burn in hell, no allowance, no supper for a week, and the doctors telling them that it's the most fatal disease of the century... I think you could produce a large number of measles deaths.

Instead the child is kept at home, given ginger ale, jello, and chicken soup, and reassured by a loving mother, whom they trust absolutely, that it's nothing serious and will go away in a few days—and it does.

Our problem is that we are all alone in the cruelest of cruel societies with no one we love and trust absolutely.

All we really need is bread, water, love, and work that we enjoy and are good at, and an undying faith in and love of ourselves, our freedom and our dignity. All that stuff is practically free, so how come it's so hard to get—and how come all these assholes and "professionals," friends and foes, family and complete strangers are always trying to convince us to follow their dumb rules, give up work in order to be a client of theirs, give up our freedom and dignity to increase their power and control?

I still don't want you to visit me here. I'm much worse, visually, than when you saw me last, so until I'm feeling stronger and looking better, let's leave it this way.

I hope this letter finds you in good spirits. I hope you're not upset that I don't want you to visit me. I wish you happiness, love, prosperity, and a limitless future.

I KNOW, I KNOW, I KNOW that somewhere there is a paradise and although I think it's really far away, I KNOW, I KNOW, I KNOW I'm gonna get there, and when I do, you're gonna be one of the first people I'll send a postcard to with complete description of, and map for locating...

Courage, bread, and roses,
Gordon

Cookie Mueller

Cookie Mueller starred in two of John Waters's films, *Pink Flamingoes* and *Female Trouble,* and in numerous Off Off Broadway productions, including her portrayal of Sharon Tate in *The Roman Polanski Story*.

She wrote the column "Ask Dr. Mueller" for the *East Village Eye* for many years, and served as art critic for *Details* and *Bomb* magazines.

Her novella *Fan Mail, Frank Letters and Crank Calls* was published in 1989. She also wrote the text for a book of drawings by her husband, Vittorio Scarpati, an artist who died of AIDS in September of 1989.

Cookie Mueller died of AIDS in November of 1989. She is survived by her son Max.